88 TIPS ON

IMMIGRATION TO CANADA

Visa, eTA, Work Permit, Study Permit, Immigration, and Citizenship to Canada

AL PARSAI, MA, DTM, RCIC

Regulated Canadian Immigration Consultant

Ashton College Instructor in Immigration Consulting Diploma

The Global School of Corporate Excellence Instructor

Copyright © 2019 Al Parsai

All rights reserved. No part of this publication may be reproduced, distributed, or transmitted in any form or by any means, including photocopying, recording, or other electronic or mechanical methods, without the prior written permission of Al Parsai, except in the case of brief quotations embodied in critical reviews and certain other non-commercial uses permitted by copyright law. For permission requests, write to Al Parsai, addressed "Attention: Permissions Coordinator," at al@parsai.ca.

ISBN: 9781791575786

DEDICATION

If I have made it this far in life is because of a wonderful woman, Golshid. You have been my companion all the way. You have been my reason to work hard and be the person I am today. I dedicate this book to you.

TABLE OF CONTENTS

Acknowledgements i
Introduction 1

PART ONE: THE BASICS 3
Tip # 01:   Five Fun Facts about Canada 4
Tip # 02:   Canadian Government(s)? 8
Tip # 03:   Canadian Currency 12
Tip # 04:   Options for Immigration to Canada 14
Tip # 05:   Who is a Canadian Citizen? 20
Tip # 06:   Who is a Permanent Resident of Canada? 22
Tip # 07:   Who is a Foreign National to Canada? 25
Tip # 08:   What is IRPA? What is IRPR? 27
Tip # 09:   IRCC - Immigration, Refugees and Citizenship Canada 28
Tip # 10:   Port of Entry 30
Tip # 11:   RCIC vs. Immigration Lawyer 32
Tip # 12:   Do I Need to Give Biometrics? 35
Tip # 13:   Canada Visa Lottery Program 38
Tip # 14:   How to Get a Visit Visa to Canada (TRV) 40
Tip # 15:   What is an eTA? 42
Tip # 16:   National Occupational Classification (NOC) 44
Tip # 17:   Some Acronyms 49
Tip # 18:   Definition of Full-time Work Experience 52
Tip # 19:   Application Status 55
Tip # 20:   Register a Business in Canada 57

PART TWO: IMMIGRATION TO CANADA 63
Tip # 21:   Economic Immigration 64
Tip # 22:   Express Entry Immigration to Canada 67

Tip # 23:	The Minimum Requirements for the Federal Skilled Worker Program	70
Tip # 24:	Federal Skilled Worker Program – Point System	74
Tip # 25:	Canadian Experience Class	79
Tip # 26:	Federal Skilled Trades Program	83
Tip # 27:	List of Jobs for the Federal Skilled Trades Program	88
Tip # 28:	Job Offer for Express Entry	94
Tip # 29:	Low-Income Cut-Off Table (LICO)	97
Tip # 30:	Federal Self-employed Program	99
Tip # 31:	Immigration to Canada for Athletes, Coaches, and Athletic Events Organizers	101
Tip # 32:	Immigration to Canada for Artists, Performers, and Self-employed People in Cultural Activities	105
Tip # 33:	The Start-up Visa Immigration	109
Tip # 34:	Designated Organizations for the Start-up Visa Immigration	114
Tip # 35:	Two-Stage Immigration for Other Self-employed and Entrepreneurs	119
Tip # 36:	Immigration under the Provincial Nominee Program	122
Tip # 37:	Family Reunification	125
Tip # 38:	Spouse, Conjugal and Common-law Partner	128
Tip # 39:	Can I Sponsor My Spouse (Wife/Husband) to Immigrate to Canada?	132
Tip # 40:	Who is a Spousal Sponsor for Immigration to Canada?	134
Tip # 41:	Immigration of Parents to Canada via Sponsorship	136
Tip # 42:	Minimum Necessary Income for Sponsoring Parents	139
Tip # 43:	Sponsoring Siblings (Brothers or Sisters) to Canada	141
Tip # 44:	Refugees and People in Need of Protection	143
Tip # 45:	Resettlement to Canada	145
Tip # 46:	Claiming Refugee Status	147
Tip # 47:	Humanitarian and Compassionate Grounds	150

PART THREE: WORKING IN CANADA 155

- Tip # 48: Work in Canada without a Permit, Legally! 156
- Tip # 49: LMIA Process and Types 159
- Tip # 50: Work in Canada without an LMIA 162
- Tip # 51: Three Steps to Work in Canada 167
- Tip # 52: Work Permit and Immigration Options for Artists 170
- Tip # 53: Work Permit for Francophones 174
- Tip # 54: Job Search Websites 178
- Tip # 55: Cold Calling for Job Search 181
- Tip # 56: USMCA (NAFTA 2.0) 184
- Tip # 57: Work Permit for Television and Film Production Workers 188
- Tip # 58: Work Permit for Successful People 190
- Tip # 59: A Special Work Permit for Performing Artists under Reciprocity 193
- Tip # 60: Business Visitors to Canada 197
- Tip # 61: Invitation Letter for Business Visitors 201
- Tip # 62: Open Work Permit 204

PART FOUR: STUDYING IN CANADA 207

- Tip # 63: Study Permit for International Students 208
- Tip # 64: Designated Learning Institutions 212
- Tip # 65: Applying for Study Permit at a Port of Entry 215
- Tip # 66: Applying for Study Permit within Canada 220
- Tip # 67: The Study Direct Stream (SDS) Program 222
- Tip # 68: Community Colleges versus Private Colleges 224
- Tip # 69: The Best Universities in Canada 228
- Tip # 70: Studying in Canada as a Minor (Primary and High School) 230
- Tip # 71: Working while Studying in Canada 234
- Tip # 72: Post-Graduate Work Permit 237

PART 5:	IMMIGRATION ISSUES	241
Tip # 73:	Removal Orders – Deportation, Exclusion, Departure	242
Tip # 74:	Authorization to Return to Canada	245
Tip # 75:	Canadian Immigration Courts and Administrative Tribunals	248
Tip # 76:	Stay Beyond Six Months in Canada	252
Tip # 77:	Driving Under the Influence	257
Tip # 78:	Five Options to Visa or Immigration Applications Refusals	260
Tip # 79:	TRP – Temporary Resident Permit to Canada	264
Tip # 80:	Misrepresentation	268
Tip # 81:	Who is Inadmissible to Canada?	271
Tip # 82:	Medical Inadmissibility to Canada	274
PART SIX:	SETTLING IN CANADA	279
Tip # 83:	Canada Day – A Reminder of Canadian Citizenship	280
Tip # 84:	Canadian Banks and Credit Unions	283
Tip # 85:	Vocational Training in Ontario	286
Tip # 86:	Sample Canadian Resumes	290
Tip # 87:	Social Insurance Number	292
Tip # 88:	Canada Sales Taxes - GST, PST, RST, and HST	294
About Parsai Immigration Services		297

ACKNOWLEDGEMENTS

It seems a cliché, but there is no doubt a book can turn into a real book due to the dedication of many. I must thank my clients for being a force for researching the immigration law. I must thank my students at Ashton College to inspire me with their questions. I also must thank my employees at Parsai Immigration Services for their questions and curiosity. Mehdi Pourian designed the cover for me. I can't thank him enough. Sepideh Razi has designed those unique cartoons for each part of the book. I will be grateful to her forever. I also need to thank my wife and children for bearing with me while I worked hard to make this book happen.

DISCLAIMER

This book does not offer official legal or immigration advice. It explains topics in general and does not apply to individual cases. Due to the time-sensitivity of immigration, the content may not be up-to-date. I cannot be held responsible for the content of this book. Please consult other resources such as an immigration lawyer or consultant or the IRCC website before deciding.

All the characters in the Tips are fictional, unless otherwise clearly stated. Any resemblance in names, dates, and places (whether individuals, organizations, regions, or countries) is coincidental.

INTRODUCTION

Once upon a time, you could immigrate to Canada by boarding a ship destined to Halifax or another major pier. A group of immigration officers greeted you at the pier and interviewed you to see if they could allow you to the country. The worst thing you usually faced, was a few days in quarantine.

Those good old days are over. The current immigration law is so complex that even some of the practitioners do not know it properly. We, nowadays, have to deal with issues such as inadmissibility, removal orders, detention due to immigration matters and more.

Immigration to Canada is my daily practice. I deal with many applicants from several countries. I see the problems they go through daily. That's why I decided to publish this book to help everyone have a better understanding of the immigration process. I originally published the tips as articles on our website settler.ca, and then I realized there are so many of them that people may get lost. This book is a collection of those articles. If you want to keep up-to-date, make sure to visit 88tips.ca from time to time. I publish any updates related to this book on that website.

There is no specific order in reading this book. Pick any Tip you like and read it. Most of the Tips are two or three pages. They are easy to read. I have also added a short story to the beginning of each Tip. I hope the stories make them more enjoyable and elaborate on the purpose of each Tip.

I have divided the book into six major parts to make it easier to navigate. The parts include,

> Part One – The Basics
>
> Part Two – Immigration to Canada
>
> Part Three – Working in Canada
>
> Part Four – Studying in Canada
>
> Part Five – Immigration Issues
>
> Part Six – Settling in Canada

The title of these parts is self-explanatory. If you are interested in working in Canada, then make sure you read Part One and Three. If you want to know about immigration to Canada, then read Part One and Two. Of course, Part Six is useful for everyone who stays in Canada. Part Five includes some advanced topics such as inadmissibility and removal orders. I enjoy that part the most, but it is up to you whether to read it or no. In spite of all these divisions, it won't hurt if you read the book cover to cover.

I must emphasize this book does not offer official immigration or legal advice. I have done my best to be as accurate as possible, but the immigration law and rules change very quickly. Some of the topics may become outdated before you know it. Also, your circumstances could affect how the regulations apply to you. Consequently, make sure to consult with official sources for decision-making.

I always welcome your feedback. You can easily find me on social media. Feel free to contact me with your valuable comments. I hope you enjoy this book.

Al Parsai – Toronto – March 2019

PART ONE:
THE BASICS

TIP # 01: FIVE FUN FACTS ABOUT CANADA

Akinyi is a young Kenyan citizen. She recently celebrated her 22nd birthday just a few days after graduating from her undergrad studies. She has the dream to travel to other places and possibly to immigrate to another country. Akinyi has heard Canada is a great destination for tourists, foreign workers, and immigrants. She, however, has no idea about Canada. Being a smart young lady, Akinyi decides to read all the tips on "88 Tips on Immigration to Canada".

Canada is an interesting country. It is probably the most welcoming country to the immigrants. Canada accepts more than 330,000 new immigrants every year. But how much do you know about Canada? This tip introduces five fun facts about Canada. I hope you enjoy them all.

FUN FACT # 1: CANADA IS THE SECOND LARGEST COUNTRY ON EARTH!

Canada is the second largest country in the world. Here is the list of top 5 countries of the world with their areas and population:

Rank	Country	Area km² (mi²)[1]	Population[2]
1	Russia	17,098,246 (6,601,670)	143,964,709
2	Canada	9,984,670 (3,855,100)	36,953,765
3	China	9,596,961 (3,705,407)	1,415,045,928
4	United States	9,525,067 (3,677,649)	326,766,748
5	Brazil	8,515,767 (3,287,956)	210,867,954

As you can see, Canada is the second largest country regarding area but the 38th country regarding population. No wonder, it needs immigrants.

FUN FACT # 2: CANADA HAS TWO OFFICIAL LANGUAGES AND MANY NON-OFFICIAL ONES!

Canada has two official languages; French and English. Most Canadians consider their first official language to be English. Since Canada is an immigration oasis, many Canadians also speak other languages. According to +Babble Magazine[3], about 58.1% of Canadians are English native speakers, 21.4% are French native speakers, and 3.5% Chinese (Mandarin or Cantonese) native speakers. The other popular languages in Canada include Spanish, Arabic, Italian, German and Urdu. About 18.8% of Canadians are native speakers in languages other than English, French or Chinese.

FUN FACT # 3: CANADA IS COLD!

If you search the internet, you quickly realize that Canada is among the top 10 coldest countries in the World on most of the lists. January is the coldest month of the year. You can hardly find a city in Canada in which the average January temperature is above the freezing point of water (i.e. 0°C or 32°F). Sometimes the temperature reaches below -40°C (-40°F).

The warmest community of Canada is Kamloops in British Columbia with an average annual high temperature of 14.8°C (58.6°F) and the average January low temperature of −5.9°C (21.4°F). The coldest community of Canada is Resolute in Nunavut with an average annual high temperature of −12.7°C (9.1°F) and the average January low temperature of −35.3°C (−31.5°F)[4].

Did I tell you, Canada neighbours the North Pole?

FUN FACT # 4: THREE OCEANS SURROUND CANADA!

Depending on who you ask, our earth has four or five oceans, namely; the Atlantic, the Pacific, the Indian, the Arctic, and the Southern (Antarctic). Three of these oceans surround Canada; the Atlantic to the east, the Arctic to the North, and the Pacific to the west. Canada borders the US to the south, but there are four mighty lakes between them, called the Great Lakes, namely; Lake Ontario, Lake Erie, Lake Huron, and Lake Superior. These are all freshwater lakes. Lake Superior is the largest freshwater lake in the world with an area of 82,100 km^2 (31,700 mi^2) and a maximum depth of 406.3 m (1,333 ft)[5].

FUN FACT # 5: CANADIANS HAVE WON THE NOBEL PRIZE 25 TIMES!

Canadians are seriously active in the field of science, literature, and world peace. So far 25 Canadians may call themselves Nobel laureates. Here is the list[6]:

- Chemistry
    - Sidney Altman
    - William Giauque
    - Gerhard Herzberg
    - Rudolph A. Marcus
    - John Polanyi
    - Michael Smith
    - Henry Taube
- Physiology or Medicine

- o Frederick Banting
- o David H. Hubel
- o Charles Brenton Huggins
- o John James Rickard Macleod
- o Ralph M. Steinman
- o Jack W. Szostak
- Literature
  - o Saul Bellow
  - o Alice Munro
- Physics
  - o Willard Boyle
  - o Bertram Brockhouse
  - o Arthur B. McDonald
  - o Donna Strickland
  - o Richard E. Taylor
- Economic Sciences
  - o Robert Mundell
  - o Myron Scholes
  - o Michael Spence
  - o William Vickrey
- Peace
  - o Lester B. Pearson

It feels good to be Canadian, eh?!!!

---

[1] https://en.wikipedia.org/wiki/List_of_countries_and_dependencies_by_area
[2] http://www.worldometers.info/world-population/population-by-country/
[3] https://www.babbel.com/en/magazine/most-spoken-languages-in-canada/
[4] https://en.wikipedia.org/wiki/Temperature_in_Canada
[5] https://en.wikipedia.org/wiki/List_of_lakes_by_area
[6] https://en.wikipedia.org/wiki/Category:Canadian_Nobel_laureates

TIP # 02: CANADIAN GOVERNMENT(S)?

Ashkan is an Iranian citizen who wishes to immigrate to Canada. He has studied different immigration options to Canada. Ashkan's intention to migrate is to find an alternative place to live that offers him many opportunities. He truly believes he needs to know more about the political system of his potential new home. Ashkan wants to know more about the Canadian government and how it is structured.

The political system of this world has divided the earth into several countries. The governments of these countries try to protect their citizens against others as much as possible. Canada is no exception. If foreigners work in our country freely, they may compromise the livelihood of Canadian citizens.

If people immigrate to Canada without proper screening, they could jeopardize our safety or security. Immigrants, visitors, foreign workers, and international students may affect Canadian culture and language significantly, to the point that it could replace our values with the ones that we don't like.

This way of thinking may seem to be xenophobic or rather fear of foreigners. Majority of Canadian people hold a moderate view of foreign nationals though. I don't think they qualify for this term. Nonetheless, most people want the government to set limitations on the influx of foreign nationals to Canada. The entity who is responsible for managing the flow of immigration is the government of Canada.

THE GOVERNMENT OF CANADA

Canada is a sovereign country. In other words, the Canadian government has the authority to make decisions about its own country without the interference of other countries. The Canadian people have chosen to call the Queen of England (and her heirs) as the head of their state. In this capacity, the Queen calls herself the Queen of Canada rather than the Queen of England. None of the other members of the British government have authority or responsibility for Canadians. The Queen of Canada appoints and delegates her duties to the Governor General who acts like the King or the Queen of Canada. For example, if the president of the United States visits Canada, it is the Governor General who typically welcomes him to our country.

The Canadian government consists of three major branches. The Legislative branch creates federal laws. The Executive branch creates and maintains policies and procedures to execute those laws. The Judiciary branch makes sure that no organization or person violates those laws.

THE LEGISLATIVE BRANCH

Canadian Parliament is the legislative branch of our country. It consists of three major parts. Governor General sits on top. The second part is the Senate which includes a group of politicians called senators. The third part is the House of Commons. People of Canada elect the members of the House of Commons through a relatively complicated election process. We call every one of these legislators as a Member of the Parliament or an MP.

THE EXECUTIVE BRANCH

Think about a running race. A group of people decide the length of the track, whether the runners can take energy enhancing drugs, the rules that disqualify a runner, and the conditions under which they may cancel the race. This group is like the legislative branch of the government. A second group decides on the qualifications of those who register the timing of the runners, the location of the hydration stations, the type and meaning of the signs they will install on the route, and so on. This group is like the executive branch of the government.

There are times that some of the people who serve in group number one (i.e. the legislative branch) also take part in group number two (i.e. the executive branch). Canadian government resembles this situation.

Canada has some federal political parties. The most powerful ones are the Liberal Party of Canada, the Conservative Party of Canada, and the New Democratic Party of Canada. Another federal party, the Green Party of Canada is gradually gaining power. These political parties introduce their candidates for every region of Canada (also called a riding) every four years or so. People vote for their Candidates through secret ballots. Every riding elects a new Member of Parliament (MP) or re-elects the old one. When the voting is completed, the political party who has the greatest number of MPs shapes the government of Canada. In other words, MPs shape the House of Commons which is a significant part of the legislative branch, and then the winning party shapes the executive branch.

The executive branch in Canada is rooted in the legislative branch. The leader of the winning political party becomes the Prime Minister of Canada. He selects some of the MPs as his cabinet. I say he, because with one exception all Canadian Prime Ministers have been men so far.

The Prime Minister (PM) has the freedom to select any MP as his cabinet members. It is not customary for the Prime Minister to cross the aisle and choose his cabinet members from the other parties though. The cabinet members become our Ministers. They oversee the government departments, or rather the agencies that draft policies and execute them. The policies of these departments must be in line with the laws passed by the legislative and judicial branch.

THE JUDICIAL BRANCH

Do you remember the running race example? What if a runner claims another runner hit her, and that's why she couldn't cross the finish line? The third group of people get involved in making decisions on situations of this nature. This group in our country is called the judicial branch. The judicial branch consists of courts and judges. This branch is independent of the legislative and executive branches to ensure the integrity of our judicial system.

Canadian judicial system consists of three major sectors. The military courts are responsible for offences with the armed forces of Canada. The provincial tribunals and courts make decisions on matters that can be resolved at the provincial level. The federal courts deal with national issues. Immigration usually falls under the federal sector.

The courts within each sector appear on different levels. The lowest level in federal courts are the federal administrative tribunals. These are specialized decision makers. Their scope of practice is limited. The largest administrative tribunal in Canada is the Immigration and Refugee Board of Canada (IRB). They have branches from coast to coast. They make decisions on matters such as inadmissibility to Canada, family sponsorship refusals, refugee claims, and detentions due to violating the immigration laws. We call the IRB judges, (panel) members.

The Federal Court is one level higher than the federal tribunals. The Federal Court of Appeal is one level higher than the Federal Court. You may appeal the decisions of Federal Court to this court under certain conditions. The highest rank court in Canada is the Supreme Court of Canada (SCC). It has the power to overrule any decisions made by any court in the country. SCC consists of nine judges. If these judges make a decision, no one can overrule it.

The Canadian judicial system is a common law system. The only exception is Quebec which uses civil law. In a common law system if a judge makes a decision the lower courts need to make the same decision under the same circumstances. In other words, if the SCC makes a decision all courts in Canada has no choice but to rule according to that decision. Even if they don't, a higher court will overturn their decisions. That's why the decisions of SCC are as powerful as the laws of the Parliament. In other words, the Canadian laws come from two sources, the legislative branch and the judicial branch.

THE THREE LEVELS OF THE GOVERNMENT IN CANADA

Canada consists of ten provinces and three territories. Each Canadian province has its government. Canadian provinces may have their own legislative, executive, and judicial branches. The authority of a provincial government is limited to their province. If a matter affects the national interest, then the federal government needs to intervene or take it under control. For example, provinces may have their police force, but the army is a federal entity.

Each province consists of several smaller regions or municipalities. These regions may have their governments. The authority of municipal governments is minimal, but it could affect the people who live in that municipality.

The ultimate decision-maker on immigration applications is the federal government of Canada. Regardless, the provinces have a say in selecting their immigrants via the Provincial Nominee Programs (PNP).

TIP # 03: CANADIAN CURRENCY

Nobel is a Citizen of Botswana. He intends to travel to Canada next month. He is preparing himself for the trip. Nobel doesn't know anything about the Canadian currency. He knows most vendors in Canada accept the US dollar, but he wants to prevent them from taking advantage of him.

Canadian unit of currency is called the Canadian Dollar. A common name for Canadian Dollar among economists and Canadian people is Loonie derived from Common Loon the name of a bird that its image appears on the face of Canadian one-dollar coins. Another common name for the Canadian dollar is a buck. Hudson's Bay Company (HBC) struck a coin in the 17th century with a value equal to the pelt of a male beaver or rather a "buck." The term remained as slang referring to the unit of currency and now refers to both Canadian and US dollars. A Canadian dollar is divided into 100 cents.

CANADIAN COINS

The following coins are widely used in Canada.

Nickel = 5 cents

Dime = 10 cents

Quarter = 25 cents

Loonie = 1 dollar or rather 100 cents

Toonie = 2 dollars

Penny or rather 1 cent coin was discontinued on February 4, 2013. The word Toonie is derived from combining the words Two and Loonie. Fifty cent coins are issued in limited edition. You may rarely find them in everyday transactions. You may, however, find 50 cents (half a dollar) coins in commemorative collections.

CANADIAN BANKNOTES

Canadian paper money which is called banknotes or notes is commonly offered in 5-dollar, 10-dollar, 20-dollar, 50-dollar, and 100-dollar denominations. It is not common to encounter a $500 note which is the highest valued banknote issued in Canada.

Most ATMs (Automated Teller Machines) also known as ABMs (Automated Banking Machines) carry $20 notes only. Some offer $50 notes as well.

Many Canadian stores do not accept $100 and $50 notes. If you carry a large banknote, you may refer to a nearby bank to convert it into smaller ones.

THE VALUE OF CANADIAN DOLLAR

The standard symbol for the Canadian dollar is CAD, but the use of $ is also quite common.

Historically, the value of the Canadian dollar has been between 0.68 USD dollar to 1.06 USD. In other words, you could sell a US dollar anywhere between 0.94 CAD to 1.45 CAD, depending on the daily exchange rate. If you visit the following link, it will redirect you to the Bank of Canada daily exchange rate page.

settler.ca/b/exchange

A US dollar was 1.33 CAD or rather a Canadian dollar was 0.75 USD at the time of writing this tip.

TIP # 04: OPTIONS FOR IMMIGRATION TO CANADA

Yu Yan is a 29-year-old Chinese citizen. She currently lives and works in Guangzhou. Yu Yan is a master Cantonese chef. She has mastered culinary arts both in practice and with education. Yu Yan knows English well, but she is not familiar with the French language. Her husband holds a bachelor's degree in accounting and works at a small accounting firm. They have a two-year-old daughter who is the sweetest creature in the world. Yu Yan wants to immigrate to Canada for a better life. She believes some major cities of Canada such as Toronto, Montreal, and Vancouver could offer her lots of opportunities to master her craft and become a globally renowned chef. Yu Yan wonders if there are any opportunities for her to immigrate to Canada. She wants to know the cost and length of the process.

The Pulse.ng website introduces Canada as the second-best country for immigration[7]. Despite being the second largest land mass in the world, Canada's population has recently passed the 37 million mark only. Compare this figure with other large countries such as Russia at 144 million, the US at 326 million, China at 1.4 billion, India at 1.3 billion, and Brazil at 210 million. Consequently, Canada is eager to bring in new immigrants as much as possible. For instance, the Canadian Government has decided to accept

330,800 immigrants in 2019 and increase this number to 341,000 in 2020 and 350,000 in 2021.

The Canadian immigration law is, known as IRPA (The Immigration and Refugee Protection Act), lays out the Canadian immigration principals. According to section 12 of the IRPA, immigration to Canada consists of three categories:

- Family Reunification (see Tip # 37)
- Economic Immigrants (see Tip # 21)
- Refugees (see Tip # 44)

Let's have a quick look at these options.

IMMIGRATION THROUGH FAMILY REUNIFICATION

A person who holds Permanent Residency (PR) or Citizenship of Canada may apply for their spouse, children, parents, grandparents, or other family members to become permanent residents of Canada under various family sponsorship programs. Different circumstances may apply to each of these groups.

Although family sponsorship is usually limited to the family members mentioned above, Canadians could sponsor other family members to Canada under rare circumstances. For example, under paragraph 117(1)(f) of the IRPR (Immigration and Refugee Protection Regulations), Canadians may sponsor their minor siblings who have lost both their parents. Paragraph 117(1)(g) also describes the possibility of adopting minor children in Canada.

Both the sponsor and the applicant need to meet certain criteria to receive the seal of approval from the immigration authorities.

In some situations, when the sponsor or their family members are not fully qualified for immigration, an immigration officer could approve the application under the Humanitarian and Compassionate grounds or H&C (see Tip # 47). In such cases, a child's emotional, social, cultural and physical welfare is the immigration officers' top priority.

Sometimes Canadian provinces introduce special family reunification opportunities for residents of their province.

ECONOMIC IMMIGRATION TO CANADA

Applicants who immigrate through the Economic classes are mainly skilled workers, business owners, or senior managers with management experience and investment capabilities. Economic immigration covers Canada's largest group of immigrants and consists of three main groups:

- **Federal** – These immigrants may settle in any province or territory of Canada other than Quebec.
- **Provincial Nominee Program (PNP)** – The applicants immigrate to a specific province of Canada other than Quebec
- **Quebec** – The province of Quebec holds a special agreement with the federal government, also known as the Quebec Accord, in which the province has the sole responsibility for its immigration programs.

IMMIGRATION UNDER THE FEDERAL PROGRAMS

The following programs are available through federal immigration:

- **Express Entry or EE** – The government introduced this system in 2015. However, it went through an overhaul in 2017, and includes three groups of immigration programs, namely:
    - The Federal Skilled Worker Program (see Tip # 23)
    - The Canadian Experience Class Program (see Tip # 25)
    - The Federal Skilled Trades Program (see Tip # 26)
- **Self-Employed program** – This program covers two specific groups, namely:
    - Athletics – Athletes and people active in sports' fields (coaches, referees, sports managers, etc.) (see Tip # 31)
    - Cultural Activities – Artists and people active in artistic and cultural fields (authors, musicians, filmmakers, screenwriters, artistic painters, singers, etc.) (see Tip # 32)
- **Start-up Visa** – This program is designed for innovative immigrants (see Tip # 33)
- **Caregivers Immigration** – This process is specific to applicants who were present and worked in Canada as caregivers.

- **Atlantic Immigration Pilot** – This program mainly targets people who have job offers from an employer in one of the Atlantic provinces, New Brunswick, Nova Scotia, Prince Edward Island, or Newfoundland and Labrador.

PNP AND QUEBEC PROGRAMS

Canada has ten provinces and three territories. Except for Nunavut, every province and territory in Canada offers some immigration opportunities. Canadian Constitution Act 1867 enables provinces to manage immigration to their province if it is not against the decisions of the Federal Government (see Tip # 36).

REFUGEES

Some people are displaced from their home countries and could be resettled to Canada as Convention refugees (see Tip # 45). When these people land in Canada, they become permanent residents of Canada. Some people come to Canada and file for asylum at a port of entry or inside Canada (see Tip # 46). Most of these people attend a hearing at the Immigration and Refugee Board of Canada. If they succeed, they may eventually become permanent residents of Canada (see Tip # 06).

OTHER WAYS TO MOVE TO CANADA

You may enter or live in Canada for a few days to several months under the following options.

- Temporary Resident Visa (see Tip # 14)
- Temporary Resident Permit (see Tip # 79)
- Study Permit (see Tip # 63)
- Work Permit (see Tip # 51)
- Work without a Permit (see Tip # 48)
- Business Visitors to Canada (see Tip # 60)

These temporary options do not necessarily result in permanent residency, but they could help. For instance, if a person works in Canada for at least one year, they may be able to apply for immigration under the Canadian Experience Class. Also, if a person finishes post-secondary level studies (i.e. master's degree or Ph.D.) in Ontario, they could apply for permanent residency under the Ontario Immigrant Nominee Program.

COST OF IMMIGRATION TO CANADA

If you intend to immigrate to Canada, consider the following costs:

- **Processing fee** – You need to pay a processing fee to the federal or provincial governments of Canada to ask them to review your application package. The amount they charge could vary from less than $100 (Canadian funds) to thousands of dollars.

- **Consultation and representation fee** – If you hire an immigration consultant or an immigration lawyer to help you with the application process, you need to pay their professional fees which are usually a few hundred to a few thousand dollars of Canada. While consultants or lawyers do not speed up your process, they could prevent drastic mistakes that could result in misrepresentation or other issues with the application. However, make sure to select a professional and knowledgeable practitioner. An incompetent practitioner could become part of the problem instead of the solution.

- **Right of Permanent Residence Fee (RPRF)** – We also know this fee as the landing fee. The fee is currently $490 per person and applies to the principal applicant and their spouse (some exceptions apply).

- **Biometrics fee** – You need to give biometrics for immigration to Canada. The current cost of biometrics is $85 per person and a maximum of $170 per family.

- **Medical examination** – All family members need to go through a medical examination. An authorized panel physician conducts the examination. Panel physicians charge you for their services. The amount you need to pay depends on your country and the complexity of your medical issues.

- **Preparation and translation of documents** – You need to prepare several documents and translate them into English or French.

- **Other expenses** – Sometimes you need to conduct exploratory visits to Canada. You may also need to pay a good faith deposit to certain provinces. Consider other unexpected expenses such as mailing documents and travelling costs to another country or city to give biometrics or attend an interview with an immigration officer.

THE PROCESSING TIME

The government of Canada tries to limit the processing time of applications to under 12 months but in reality, the processing time of applications could exceed a few years. The processing time depends on many factors such as the method of immigration, the complexities surrounding the application, the officer who reviews the case, the visa office reviewing the case, the completeness of the package, and more.

---

[7] https://www.pulse.ng/lifestyle/food-travel/tips-these-are-the-7-best-countries-to-immigrate-to/1lb135j

TIP # 05: WHO IS A CANADIAN CITIZEN?

Kiarash was born in Ottawa, Canada in 1983. His parents were both international students from Iran. They completed their studies and left without applying for immigration. Kiarash was only four months old when his parents left Canada for good. Kiarash has never travelled to Canada and does not hold any Canadian documents other than his birth certificate. A friend of Kiarash recently told him, he is a Canadian citizen. He wonders if this is true.

Many people around the world consider Canadian citizenship a privilege. One of the reasons that people immigrate to Canada is to become Canadian citizens. They leave their home country, their language, their relatives, and sometimes their culture and beliefs behind to pursue a new life which eventually turns them into Canadian citizens.

People could become Canadians either by birth or through naturalization. The Canadian Citizenship Act calls naturalization, citizenship by way of grant.

WHO IS A CANADIAN BY BIRTH?

There are two ways that a person becomes Canadian by birth. If someone is born in Canada, then they automatically become a Canadian citizen. The only exception is when one of the parents is a foreign country employee or diplomat and the other parent is not a Canadian citizen or permanent resident of Canada.

The other option for citizenship by birth is for those people who are born outside Canada, but at least one of their parents is a first generation Canadian. You are a first generation Canadian if you are either born inside Canada or if you become a Canadian by way of naturalization.

WHO IS A NATURALIZED CITIZEN?

Simply put, a naturalized citizen is someone who immigrates to Canada first and then after a few years applies and becomes a Canadian citizen. For example, according to the existing regulations, if you are a landed immigrant and in the past five years have spent at least three years in Canada, then you may apply for citizenship. The next steps usually involve in submitting some documents, taking a citizenship test, and eventually taking the Oath of Citizenship (or rather attending the Citizenship ceremony).

Children under 18 could become naturalized citizens when their parents become Canadians.

WHAT ARE THE DIFFERENCES BETWEEN NATURALIZED AND BORN CITIZENS?

Federal and provincial laws and courts treat naturalized and born citizens equally. Both groups have similar responsibilities and privileges. Nobody in the country could treat such citizens differently. Nonetheless, there are certain differences that you need to keep in mind:

- If a naturalized citizen has obtained their permanent residency or citizenship fraudulently, then immigration authorities may revoke their citizenship.

- A naturalized citizen cannot hold a Canadian birth certificate.

- A naturalized citizen may be treated by other countries differently due to their place of birth, despite their Canadian citizenship.

TIP # 06: WHO IS A PERMANENT RESIDENT OF CANADA?

Binsa is a 26-year-old Nepali citizen. She knows both the English and French languages very well. She holds a master's degree in accounting. Binsa also has more than three years of work experience as an accountant. One of Binsa's friends, Chimini, tells her to immigrate to Canada. Chimini tells Binsa if she immigrates to Canada, she can become a Permanent Resident. Binsa wonders what permanent residency means.

A Permanent Resident (PR) of Canada may live or work anywhere in Canada. Section 6 of the Canadian Constitution Act, 1982 protects this right. Permanent residents also have the right to enter Canada under section 27 of IRPA (see Tip # 08 for more information about IRPA).

Some conditions apply to these freedoms. For example, provinces may limit the migration of people from other provinces to their own. To the best of my knowledge, such a decision has never been exercised by any provinces of Canada yet.

If a Permanent Resident commits a serious crime such as murder, membership to criminal gangs, treason, espionage, or terrorism, they may lose their PR status (see Tip # 81 for more information on inadmissibility to Canada).

Permanent Residents need to spend about 40% of their time in Canada, or they will lose their status. As a general rule, a PR needs to spend at least 730 days in a five-year cycle inside Canada to keep their permanent residency. Section 28 of IRPA offers some alternatives to physical presence in Canada, namely.

1. Accompanying a Canadian citizen outside Canada who is their spouse or common-law partner
2. Being employed full-time by a Canadian company outside Canada
3. Being employed full-time by a Canadian federal or provincial organization outside Canada
4. Accompany a spouse or common-law partner who meets the conditions of row 2 or 3 above

Of course, someone may meet a combination of these. For example, they may be present in Canada for 400 days and then be employed by a Canadian company outside Canada for another 330 days outside Canada.

HOW TO BECOME A PERMANENT RESIDENT

As you may have guessed, you need to immigrate to Canada to become a Permanent Resident. Read Tip # 04 (Options for Immigration to Canada) for more information about potential options for immigration.

If you successfully immigrate to Canada and stay in our country for a while you could become a Canadian Citizen (see Tip # 05 – Who is a Canadian Citizen?).

PERMANENT RESIDENT CARD

When you become a permanent resident of Canada, you receive a permanent resident or PR card. This card helps you board an airplane and travel to Canada. It also verifies your permanent residency. You usually need to renew your PR card every five years.

CONFIRMATION OF PERMANENT RESIDENCY (COPR)

Landing refers to the first time you enter Canada to become a permanent resident. When you land, you also receive a piece of paper called COPR. Hold on to this paper for the rest of your life as it is the proof you entered Canada once as a permanent resident. If you lose this paper, you may contact IRCC to issue you a copy.

TIP # 07: WHO IS A FOREIGN NATIONAL TO CANADA?

Amaya is a Dominican citizen. She recently received a 3-year work permit to Canada. Amaya intends to work for a Canadian firm in Churchill, Manitoba. She wonders what her status in Canada is.

Under the Canadian laws people are divided into three major groups:

1. Canadian Citizens (defined under sections 3 to 5 of the Citizenship Act)
   - People who are born inside Canada (conditions may apply), or
   - People who are born outside Canada whose parents are first-generation Canadian Citizens (conditions may apply), or
   - People who immigrated to Canada and later became Naturalized Citizens.
2. Permanent Residents of Canada (defined under section 12 of the Immigration and Refugee Protection Act)
   - People who have immigrated to Canada under any of the family reunification programs, or

- People who have immigrated to Canada under any of the economic immigration programs, or
- People who have immigrated to Canada as refugees.

3. Foreign Nationals

Under subsection 2(1) of the Immigration and Refugee Protection Act of Canada (IRPA) "foreign national means a person who is not a Canadian citizen or a permanent resident and includes a stateless person."

Some examples of foreign nationals include,

- International students
- Temporary foreign workers
- International tourists
- Foreign business visitors
- Foreign diplomats
- People who are in Canada without proper documents (i.e. illegal residents or stateless residents)

The state of being a Citizen, Permanent Resident, or Foreign National is independent of the location of a person. In other words, a Canadian citizen remains a citizen whether they live inside Canada or outside Canada. A permanent resident of Canada remains a permanent resident unless they lose their permanent residency because of inadmissibility issues (e.g. due to terrorism or serious crimes) or they do not meet their residency requirements (under section 28 of the IRPA).

A permanent resident who loses their permanent residency becomes a foreign national. A citizen who loses their citizenship may become a permanent resident or a foreign national, depending on the circumstances that resulted in the loss or renunciation of citizenship.

TIP # 08: WHAT IS IRPA? WHAT IS IRPR?

Lucas is a law professor in Denmark. He recently initiated researching the Canadian legal system. Lucas wants to know more about the laws that govern the Canadian immigration system. He needs to know their names before delving into more details about them.

IRPA stands for the Immigration and Refugee Protection Act. It refers to the Act of the Canadian Parliament that builds the foundation for immigration policies, processes, and procedures. It also defines matters such as immigration offences, temporary resident to Canada, permanent residency, refugee claims, inadmissibility to Canada and more. In this book, I may refer to the provisions of IRPA by the letter A. For example, A24 means section 24 of IRPA.

IRPR stands for the Immigration and Refugee Protection Regulations. Under IRPA the Minister of IRCC has the authority to develop certain rules to expand on IRPA. Such rules further offer details about the immigration process in Canada. For example, the location you may apply for a Work Permit, or who may study in Canada without a study permit, and so on. In this book, I may refer to the provisions of IRPR by the letter R. For example, R24 means section 24 of IRPR.

TIP # 09: IRCC - IMMIGRATION, REFUGEES AND CITIZENSHIP CANADA

Adya is a citizen of Djibouti. She is 18 years old. Adya recently finished her high school. She wants to continue her studies in Canada. Adya's friend told her she needs to visit the IRCC website for more information about her options. She wonders what does IRCC mean.

IRCC stands for Immigration, Refugees and Citizenship Canada. You may know this organization as CIC or rather Citizenship and Immigration Canada. The government of Canada replaced CIC with IRCC in 2015. It is good to know that IRCC is responsible for the following activities.

- Setting policies and procedures for immigration to Canada
- Reviewing immigration applications and making decisions on them
- Issuing permanent resident visas and cards
- Setting policies and procedures for temporary residency (e.g. TRV, TRP, Study Permit, Work Permit)
- Reviewing temporary residency applications and making

decisions on them

- Dealing with refugee applications inside and outside Canada
- Reviewing citizenship applications and granting citizenship
- Issuing passports and other travel documents (e.g. travel documents for refugees)

ORGANIZATIONS CLOSE TO IRCC

Many organizations in Canada work closely with IRCC, but the following are some of the most important ones.

- **CBSA (Canada Border Services Agency)** – This organization is the policing force for immigration. It also provides lawyers for IRCC when someone files a lawsuit (Judicial Review) against the Immigration Minister.
- **IRB (Immigration and Refugee Board of Canada)** – This organization is an administrative tribunal (similar to a court). It makes decisions on matters such as inadmissibility to Canada or refugee applications in Canada (see Tip # 75).
- **CSIS (Canadian Security Intelligence Service)** – CSIS is the Canada spying agency. They help with the security screening of immigration and visa applicants.

Many other organizations such as **RCMP (the federal police of Canada)** or **Global Affairs Canada** (the department of foreign affairs) also work hand in hand with IRCC to protect the integrity of our immigration system.

THE IRCC WEBSITE

The old IRCC website was www.cic.gc.ca. You may still some pages of the IRCC on the old website. The new website is part of canada.ca.

TIP # 10: PORT OF ENTRY

Imeda is a citizen of Georgia. He holds a visitor's visa from the US and another one from Canada. Imeda is currently in Detroit, Michigan. He has heard no army or barrier to protect the border between the United States and Canada. Considering holding a valid visa to Canada, Imeda wonders if he can cross the border at any point.

Port of entry (POE) is where you may legally cross the border of a country. You may not cross the Canadian border other than through a POE. Canadian ports of entry include the following:

- **Some Canadian airports** such as Toronto Pearson International Airport, Montréal-Pierre Elliott Trudeau International Airport, Vancouver International Airport, and Halifax Stanfield International Airport

- **Land ports** of entry where you may cross with a vehicle or in some cases on foot, such as Windsor – Ambassador Bridge, Niagara Falls – Rainbow Bridge, Boundary Bay (British Columbia), Scobey–Coronach Border Crossing (Saskatchewan), and Chateaugay–Herdman Border Crossing (Quebec)

- **Ferry crossings** where a ferry takes you to Canada, such as Prince Rupert (British Columbia), Walpole Island (Ontario), and Yarmouth (Nova Scotia)

- **Rail crossings** where you cross the border with the help of a train, such as White Rock (British Columbia), Niagara Falls (Ontario), and Cantic (Quebec)
- **Seaports** where you enter Canada with a boat or a ship, such as Sept-Îles Port (Quebec), Belledune Port (New Brunswick), and St. John's Port (Newfoundland and Labrador)

Some of the services offered at a port of entry include:

- Examining foreign nationals and others to enter Canada
- Issuing visitor records, TRPs, study permits, or work permits
- Changing the status of an applicant (e.g. from a visitor to a permanent resident)
- Administering biometrics (see Tip # 12 for more information about biometrics)
- Running typical tasks of customs (collecting tariffs or duties, preventing certain goods from entering Canada, etc.)

The officials at a port of entry may sometimes remove a person from Canada or detain certain foreign nationals or permanent residents under the immigration law (IRPA) or other laws of Canada (see Part Five of the book for more information about such issues).

Even if you do not need a visa to enter Canada or you are a permanent resident or a citizen of Canada, you may not cross the border other than at a designated port of entry. Some ports of entry offer limited services or limited hours of operation. Make sure to double check the availability of each port of entry before making travel plans to Canada.

TIP # 11: RCIC VS. IMMIGRATION LAWYER

Anaya is a Pakistani citizen. She and her husband and children intend to immigrate to Canada. Anaya understands that immigration is a complex process and involves legal or procedural matters such as admissibility to Canada, meeting the minimum requirements, filling out several forms, preparation and submitting documents, and communication with the officials of the government of Canada. As a result, Anaya has decided to hire a professional to help her with the matter. She has heard that both an immigration consultant or an immigration lawyer may help her with the process. She wonders who she may hire.

Canada has ten provinces and three territories. Each of these provinces or territories have a law society (e.g. the Law Society of Ontario, the Nova Scotia Barristers Society, or the Law Society of British Columbia). Canadian lawyers are members of one of those law societies. Under section 91 of IRPA, a lawyer who is a member in good standing of one of the law societies in Canada may represent clients to the immigration authorities. The scope of practice for lawyers is not limited to immigration. They may, for example, deal with criminal litigation, civil lawsuits, real-estate transfers, and more. Lawyers usually take less than three subjects related to immigration at a law school while studying to become lawyers.

Another group of licensed representatives are the Regulated Canadian Immigration Consultants, also known as RCIC. An RCIC is a member of ICCRC or the Immigration Consultants of Canada Regulatory Council. According to ICCRC, a person needs to take a 500-hour approved training program and show excellent knowledge of English or French languages among other requirements to become an RCIC. Almost all the training an RCIC receives is directly related to the immigration law and practice. However, RCICs do not receive training in other fields of the law. In other words, RCICs are more into the process of immigration and lawyers in the field of litigation. Of course, some lawyers are dedicated to the immigration process as well.

The following table shows a brief list of services offered by the Lawyers and RCICs. In this table, "Yes" means a competent professional could offer the service; "Maybe" means they may need extra licenses to do the job; and "No" means the service is outside their scope of practice.

Nature of the Service	Lawyer	RCIC
Temporary Foreign Worker Program (TFWP)	Yes	Yes
Labour Market Impact Assessment (LMIA)	Yes	Yes
International Mobility Program (IMP): Visa applications under international, Canadian Interests, or humanitarian reasons	Yes	Yes
Temporary Resident Visa (TRV) for Tourists, Business Visitors, Speakers, and Performers	Yes	Yes
Temporary Resident Permit (TRP)	Yes	Yes
Electronic Travel Authorization (eTA)	Yes	Yes
Study Permit and Visa	Yes	Yes
Economic Classes (Federal Immigration)	Yes	Yes
Sponsorship Applications for Spouses, Children, Adopted Children, Parents, and other Family Members	Yes	Yes
Refugee Applications/Claims	Yes	Yes
Detention Hearings (Immigration and Refugee Board – IRB)	Yes	Yes

Nature of the Service	Lawyer	RCIC
Inadmissibility Hearings (IRB)	Yes	Yes
Immigration Appeal Division Hearings (IRB)	Yes	Yes
Refugee Protection Division and Appeal Hearings (IRB)	Yes	Yes
Representing Applicants/Travellers to the Canada Border Services Agency (CBSA)	Yes	Yes
Offering Canadian Immigration, Visa, and Citizenship Advice	Yes	Yes
Citizenship Applications	Yes	Yes
Rehabilitation applications	Yes	Yes
Authorization to Return to Canada (ARC)	Yes	Yes
Immigration, study permit and work permit to Quebec	Yes	Maybe
Judicial Review (Federal Court)	Yes	No

When you are hiring a lawyer or an immigration consultant, make sure they are competent in their field.

TIP # 12: DO I NEED TO GIVE BIOMETRICS?

Caleb is a citizen of Papua New Guinea. He intends to travel to Canada next month to visit his brother who is a Canadian citizen. Caleb has heard about biometrics to visit or immigrate to Canada, but he is not quite sure what biometrics refers to and if he needs to give biometrics.

If you want to travel to Canada, study in Canada, work in Canada, or immigrate to Canada, you may need to give biometrics. You usually refer to a Visa Application Centre (VAC). They take your fingerprints and digital photo. They use the information to check your background. They also match your picture with you when you enter Canada at a port of entry (see Tip # 10). Biometrics are necessary for the following applications:

- Immigration to Canada
- Temporary Resident Visas (TRV)
- Temporary Resident Permits (TRP)
- Study Permits
- Work Permits

If you are applying for a Work Permit or Study Permit at the Port of

Entry, then a Border Services Officer will take your biometrics and collects the biometrics fee.

Biometrics are not necessary for regular eTA applications (see Tip # 15 for more information about eTA).

WHAT ARE BIOMETRICS?

As mentioned earlier biometrics refers to digital photos and fingerprints. Most people need to give biometrics even before entering Canada. Some people need to provide biometrics at the port of entry. Regardless of the location of biometrics, a Border Services Officer may double-check your biometrics at the port of entry to make sure you are the same person who gave the biometrics. With this approach, they enhance the security and integrity of the Canadian immigration system.

VALIDITY OF BIOMETRICS

Biometrics are valid for up to 10 years. If you give biometrics for a temporary visit or stay in Canada, you may still need to provide biometrics for immigration to Canada. You may also voluntarily give biometrics before the expiry date of the current biometrics (e.g. if it is very close to the expiry of your biometrics or your looks has changed significantly due to injuries or plastic surgery).

Keep in mind, you need a letter from the immigration authorities to be able to give biometrics, or you need to give biometrics while you are handing your documents to a VAC.

BIOMETRICS FEE

The current fees for biometrics are the following. All the charges are in Canadian Dollars:

- $85 for one person
- $170 for a family of two or more
- $255 for a group of three or more performing artists

WHO IS EXEMPT FROM BIOMETRICS?

The following groups are exempt from biometrics:

- Her Majesty Queen Elizabeth II and any member of the Royal Family

- Diplomats (some exceptions and expansions exist)

- US nationals, unless they are applying for immigration to Canada

- Asylum claimants who are older than 13 (no upper age limit)

- Applicants who are not asylum claimants, but they are either younger than 14 or older than 79

- Travellers who are transiting through Canada to the United States

- Visa exempt foreign nationals who are applying for an Electronic Travel Authorization (eTA)

- Some other groups such as some visiting members of foreign armed forces

TIP # 13: CANADA VISA LOTTERY PROGRAM

Josivini is a citizen of Fiji. She desperately wants to immigrate to Canada. Josivini visited has consulted with several immigration consultants and lawyers, but they believe she does not meet the requirements of any immigration option to Canada. She recently ran into a website that promotes a lottery program to Canada. The site claims Josivini may pay a nominal fee and then enter a raffle for immigration to Canada. This opportunity seems too good to be true. She wants to investigate the matter further.

Canada is the most wanted immigration destination in the world. The diversity of the country and its reception to newcomers is exceptional. If you move to large urban areas such as Toronto, Vancouver, Montreal, or Calgary, you feel at home as you will find many people from your ethnic or cultural background. Canada accepts about 300,000 new immigrants every year. Because of these reasons, there are millions of people who are interested in immigrating to Canada every year.

The Canadian government has set particular criteria to filter out these applicants and accept immigrants based on their economic value to Canada, strengthening the social fabric of the country, or meeting the humanitarian obligations. Simply put, despite being receptive to immigrants, there are several restrictions on how they chose the immigration applicants.

Picture this! Millions of people want to immigrate to Canada every year. Only 300,000 of them or so will get through. Consequently, the immigration market to Canada is full of people who are desperate to find a way to land in Canada. Unfortunately, this environment calls for scammers and fraudsters.

Several prospects clients notified me of a fictitious program called "Canada Visa Lottery" or "Canada Immigration Lottery." Such programs do not exist. Period!

If someone approaches you about a Canadian visa or immigration lottery, please report them to the Canada Border Services Agency (CBSA). If you want to know more about legitimate immigration options to Canada, read this book thoroughly.

TIP # 14: HOW TO GET A VISIT VISA TO CANADA (TRV)

Issouf who is a citizen of Burkina Faso wants to travel to Canada to attend a three-day professional seminar. He is a civil engineer who works for the municipality of Bobo-Dioulasso. Issouf knows he needs a visitor's visa to travel to Canada, but he is not quite sure if he could get one.

Some visitors to Canada are exempt from visas or need an eTA to visit the country, but many people need a Temporary Resident Visa (TRV) to visit Canada. Not every applicant receives the visa. You need to convince an immigration officer you meet the following requirements before they issue a TRV.

- You have a valid reason for visiting Canada
- You have enough financial resources to cover the expenses of your visit
- You will return to your country of the residence before the expiry date of your visa
- You are not inadmissible to Canada (see Tip # 81)

Some examples of valid reasons for visiting Canada include visiting relatives and friends, attending seminars or exhibitions, attending concerts and other public performances, and receiving medical treatment. When you submit your TRV application, you need to provide some documents to explain why you are visiting Canada. If the purpose of your visit is unclear or shows you intend to study, work, or illegally stay in Canada, the officer will refuse your application.

The financial resources refer to the money available to you or the person who is willing to invite you to Canada. You may verify the amount via your bank statements, salary slips or other financial documents. Do some research around the potential expenses you incur during the visit. Then make sure the documents you present, verify you have enough money to cover those expenses. It is reasonable to purchase travel insurance for your trip to Canada.

The main reason for TRV refusal is when an officer is not convinced you will return to your home country or country of residence before the expiry of your visa. You need to show you have enough ties to your country of residence and have no reason to overstay in Canada. Emotional, familial, and financial ties are among the most convincing reasons. Make sure to offer credible documents. For example, if your company provides you with a three-week leave and they may fire you if you do not go back to work in a timely fashion get an official letter from them on their letterhead. Include all these documents in your application package.

A rich history of travelling to other countries is a good indication you do not want to stay in Canada illegally. If you show you have gone to other countries recently, make sure to present relevant documents to the immigration officer (e.g. visa counterfoils, entry and exit stamps, etc.).

The officer may refuse the application because the applicant is inadmissible to Canada due to medical reasons, criminality, security or terrorism, or organized crime. If you are in doubt that you may be inadmissible to Canada contact a Regulated Canadian Immigration Consultant (RCIC) or a Canadian immigration lawyer for advice (see Tip # 11 for the difference between and RCIC and a lawyer).

Officers are trained to process the applications fairly. However, there is a considerable degree of subjectivity in assessing TRV applications. In other words, depending on how the officer views your application, they decide if they issue the visa or not. If they refuse your visa on inadmissibility grounds, it is challenging to get a visa in the future. Consult with a professional about your potential options. If they reject the application on other grounds, you may submit another application with more convincing documents.

TIP # 15: WHAT IS AN ETA?

Olivia is a British citizen. She is 25 years old and lives in Manchester, UK. Olivia wants to visit Canada as a tourist. She booked her flight through a travel agency last week. Olivia later received a call about an eTA application from her travel agent. She was under the impression she does not need a visa to Canada. Olivia wonders what an eTA is and why she needs one.

Some nationalities are exempt from visas to travel to Canada. For example, if you are a US citizen and intend to visit family members or tourist attractions in Canada, you do not need a visa. You enter Canada with your US passport. A Border Services Officer (BSO) usually allows you to stay in Canada for up to six months.

The Government of Canada has made some significant changes to the visa-exemption program. Most visa exempt people need to apply for an eTA or rather an electronic Travel Authorization if they travel by air to Canada or transit via Canada to another country. The changes came into effect on March 15, 2016. US citizens do not need an eTA to go to Canada, but almost all other nationalities are not exempt from an eTA. The permanent residents of the US such as Green Card holders need an eTA for air travels to Canada.

If you are a dual Citizen of Canada, you do not need an eTA, but you need to prove you are a Canadian citizen. The easiest way to prove your citizenship is to hold a Canadian passport.

If you need a visa to travel to Canada, then you do not need an eTA. You have to apply for a Temporary Resident Visa (TRV) instead.

If you intend to work or study in Canada, then an eTA is not sufficient. You may also need to apply for a work permit or a study permit (see parts three and four of this book).

The process of applying for an eTA is relatively easy. You need to fill out an online form on the IRCC website and pay the processing fee. The current processing fee is $7.00 Canadian per applicant.

You need to apply separately for every member of the family who intends to accompany you to Canada unless they are exempt from an eTA. There is no exemption because of age.

When you apply for an eTA, you usually receive your eTA in a few minutes. Some people may receive an email from IRCC (Immigration, Refugees, and Citizenship Canada) requesting some documents. These applications may take several days or even weeks to complete, so get ready for unforeseen situations. Also, keep in mind that IRCC keeps the right to refuse eTA applications.

TIP # 16: NATIONAL OCCUPATIONAL CLASSIFICATION (NOC)

Aboubakar is a citizen of the Central African Republic. He is a professional accountant who intends to immigrate to Canada under the Federal Skilled Worker program. Aboubakar has heard, his work needs to be a NOC Type 0, A, or B to be able to apply for immigration. He has no idea what NOC is and what those types are.

Under section 12 of the Canadian immigration law (IRPA), immigrants fall into three groups of family reunion, economic immigrants, and refugees. About half of the newcomers immigrate to Canada under the economic programs. Majority of these programs rely on the skills and job experiences of these applicants. Canada welcomes most job experiences. However, depending on your job experience and skills, your options for immigration vary. That's why you need to know how the Canadian government looks at your job experience.

The organization that oversees human resources in Canada is ESDC or rather Employment and Social Development Canada. ESDC classifies jobs in Canada into more than 500 categories. Each category has a four-digit code. For example, code 7611 refers to "Construction trades helpers and labourers." This code covers a large group of job titles, such as demolition workers, drywall sanders, concrete mixer helpers, and bricklayer helpers, among others.

This code and other ESDC four-digit codes fall under a system called *National Occupational Classification* or *NOC*. The NOC system is a method to define and understand the nature, duties, and requirements of every single occupation in Canada.

SKILL LEVELS OR TYPES UNDER NOC

Under NOC, skill types refer to the nature of the occupation and include ten categories, namely:

- Skill Type 0 – Management occupations
- Skill Type 1 – Business, finance and administration occupations
- Skill Type 2 – Natural and applied sciences and related occupations
- Skill Type 3 – Health occupations
- Skill Type 4 – Occupations in education, law and social, community and government services
- Skill Type 5 – Occupations in art, culture, recreation and sport
- Skill Type 6 – Sales and service occupations
- Skill Type 7 – Trades, transport and equipment operators and related occupations
- Skill Type 8 – Natural resources, agriculture and related production occupations
- Skill Type 9 – Occupations in manufacturing and utilities

NOC divides jobs into five significant skill Levels. The skill levels are based on the nature of the duties and also the level of education a person normally needs to get the job. They include the following:

- Skill Level 0 refers to managerial positions, such as chief executive officers, senior government managers, college presidents, club managers, and store managers.
- Skill Level A covers jobs that generally call for a university degree, such as financial auditors, civil engineers, human resource professionals, and physicists.

- Skill Level B refers to jobs that usually require a college diploma, such as admin assistants, event planners, insurance underwriters, plumbers, welders, and customs brokers.

- Skill Level C usually calls for a combination of a high-school diploma and job-specific training, such as transformer winders, court clerks, collectors, payroll administrators, and postal workers.

- Skill Level D refers to labour jobs that usually need on-the-job training, such as fish weighers, meat packagers, cloth carriers, and shipfitter helpers.

As you may have noticed the management occupations appear both under the skill levels and skill types. This approach is a bit confusing, but it makes sense because managerial positions are independent of the kind of the job or even the level of education you have, yet they are an integral part of the labour market.

LOCATING AND UNDERSTANDING A NOC CODE

There are many ways to determine NOC codes. The easiest one is probably to visit the "Find Your NOC" page. The following link takes you to that page:

settler.ca/88/noc

Let's say you enter "glazier helper" in the search box. You will then see the content of the following table:

NOC	Title	Skill level or type
7611	Construction trades helpers and labourers	D

The first column shows the NOC code. The second column shows the title. In an actual search result, you may click the title to view a page on the ESDC website that explains this NOC code in detail. The last column is the skill level of this code.

As mentioned earlier, if you click the title of the NOC code, you will be redirected to the ESDC page that explains this code. It includes the lead statement about the classification. If the job you are looking up does not match the lead statement, you are looking at the wrong code. Keep searching for the correct one. Of course, you may see some differences, but generally speaking, the lead statement must match the description of the job.

The "Example Titles" section follows the lead statement. If the job title you are looking up is not there, don't panic. Those are only examples. Your focus needs to be on the lead statement and the main duties sections.

The "Main Duties" section lists the main duties that describe the code. In most cases, you need to see about 70% match between the responsibilities of your job and the bullet points under this section (some exceptions may exist).

Other sections such as the Employment Requirements, Additional Information, and Exclusions are usually irrelevant to the immigration or work permit process. Nonetheless, make sure to read them and consult with a professional about their importance.

NOC AND IMMIGRATION TO CANADA

When you immigrate to Canada, you need to make sure your job experience and skills fall under the expectations for your stream of application. For example, if you are applying under the Federal Skilled Worker program (see Tip # 23), then you need to show you have at least one year of experience under a skill type 0, or a skill level A or B job in the past ten years (among other conditions). The Federal Skilled Trades program (see Tip # 26) requires skill type B jobs under NOC codes 72xx, 73xx, 82xx, 92xx, 632x, and 633x. You may replace "x" with any available number under the NOC matrix.

NOC AND WORK PERMIT TO CANADA

If you want to stay and work in Canada temporarily (i.e. for a few days to a few years), you usually need a Work Permit or rather a document issued by the Canadian immigration authorities that allows you to work in Canada. Depending on the NOC code, the nature of the job you do, your situation in Canada, and the source of remuneration you may fall under any of the following categories.

- The necessity to obtain an LMIA or rather a Labour Market Impact Assessment from ESDC that ensures your work in Canada has a positive impact on the labour market in our country. You also need a Work Permit from IRCC under this category (see Tip # 49).

- The necessity to obtain a Work Permit but exempt from an

LMIA under special programs under the International Mobility Program (see Tip # 50).

- Being exempt from both LMIA and Work Permit, for example, some business visitors, some performers, some airline crew members, or some professional or amateur athletes (see Tip # 48).

TIP # 17: SOME ACRONYMS

Safira is a citizen of Suriname. She recently decided to immigrate to Canada. To start her research, she googled "immigration to Canada." Safira visited many websites, but they all include a lot of acronyms that she doesn't understand. She eventually purchases "88 Tips on Immigration to Canada" and opens Tip # 17 to understand what those acronyms mean.

The world of immigration to Canada is full of abbreviations and acronyms. The following list shows some of those abbreviations.

Acronym	What does it represent?
BSO	Border Services Officer
	The officer you normally meet when you attempt to enter Canada through any of the borders.
CAPIC	Canadian Association of Professional Immigration Consultants
	CAPIC is the professional organization created for regulated Canadian immigration consultants (RCICs) and founded on the four pillars of education, information, lobbying, and recognition[8].

Acronym	What does it represent?
CBSA	Canada Border Services Agency
	The Canada Border Services Agency (CBSA) ensures the security and prosperity of Canada by managing the access of people and goods to and from Canada[9].
CEC	Canadian Experience Class (see Tip # 25)
CIC	Citizenship and Immigration Canada
	The previous name for IRCC.
CSIC	Canadian Society of Immigration Consultants
	Former regulator (before IRCC) for Canadian immigration consultants. The government of Canada replaced CSIC with ICCRC in 2011.
CRA	Canada Revenue Agency
	A government agency which is mostly in charge of collecting taxes and setting tax policies.
CRS	Comprehensive Ranking System
	A 1200 point-system for Express Entry applicants.
EE	Express Entry (see Tip # 22)
ESDC	Employment and Social Development Canada
	An organization that monitors the Canadian job market regulates certain aspects of employment and develops the National Occupational Classification (NOC), etc.
DLI	Designated Learning Institutions (see Tip # 64)
eTA	Electronic Travel Authorization (see Tip # 15)
FSTP	Federal Skilled Trades Program (see Tip # 26)
FSWP	Federal Skilled Worker Program (see Tip # 23)
ICCRC	Immigration Consultants of Canada Regulatory Council.
	ICCRC is the national regulatory body designated by the government of Canada in July 2011, to regulate Canadian immigration, citizenship and international student advising services. Permitted service providers of these regulated professions are known as Regulated Canadian Immigration

Acronym	What does it represent?
	Consultants (RCICs) and Regulated International Student Immigration Advisors (RISIAs)[10].
IRB	Immigration and Refugee Board of Canada
	An administrative tribunal (like a court) that deals with many refugee and immigration hearings (see Tip # 75)
IRPA	Immigration and Refugee Protection Act (see Tip # 8)
IRPR	Immigration and Refugee Protection Regulations (see Tip # 8)
IRCC	Immigration, Refugees, and Citizenship Canada was formerly known as CIC (see Tip # 9)
LICO	Low-Income Cut-Off (see Tip # 29)
NOC	National Occupational Classification (see Tip # 16)
POE	Port of Entry (see Tip #10)
RCIC	Regulated Canadian Immigration Consultant A member in good standing of ICCRC (see Tip # 11)
RCMP	Royal Canadian Mounted Police
	An acronym referring to the federal police of Canada
LMIA	Labour Market Impact Assessment (see Tip # 49)
PA	The Principal Applicant in an immigration application
SIN	Social Insurance Number (see Tip # 87)
TRP	Temporary Resident Permit (see Tip # 79)
TRV	Temporary Resident Visa (see Tip # 14)

---

[8] http://capic.ca/EN/MissionVision
[9] http://www.cbsa-asfc.gc.ca/agency-agence/menu-eng.html
[10] https://iccrc-crcic.ca/about-us/

TIP # 18: DEFINITION OF FULL-TIME WORK EXPERIENCE

Chione is an Egyptian insurance adjuster. She works on a part-time basis for a large insurance company in Cairo. Chione works part-time because she is also taking care of her two-year-old daughter. She has recently decided to immigrate to Canada, but she wonders if her part-time job counts.

If you intend to work or immigrate to Canada, an immigration officer may ask you about your full-time work experience, but what is full-time work experience?

Under the IRCC guidelines, a full-time job refers to at least 30 hours of work per week. It is okay if you take a short leave of absence for vacation or personal reasons, but that break should not interrupt your work. For example, taking a week off to visit your ailing mother is okay but taking three months off is not okay. Such gaps could affect the continuity of your work experience.

Sometimes you may work less than 30 hours a week. In these situations, you may calculate the full-time equivalent instead of actual full-time work. Let's say you work two years for a company, but you only spent 15 hours a week there. In this example, your two-year work experience is equal to one-year full-time work experience.

If you work more than 30 hours a week, you may not use the extra hours to increase your work experience duration. For example, if you work 60 hours a week for one year, you still have only one year of full-time work experience, not two years.

To verify your work experience, present the following documents.

- An employment contract
- A reference letter from your employer on their letterhead that indicates the following:
    - Your job title
    - Your job duties
    - The average number of hours you worked per week
    - The start date and the end date of your job
- Another document that verifies your contract and reference letter, for example:
    - A pay stub
    - The business card of you or your manager with the contact information
    - A reference letter from another colleague
    - A printout of your name on the company's website

This list is neither inclusive nor exclusive. You need to present enough documents to convince the officer your claim is truthful.

The IRCC sometimes accepts self-employment and sometimes doesn't. Here are some examples.

- Federal Skilled Worker Program – Acceptable
- Federal Self-employed Class – Expected and Acceptable
- Canadian Experience Class – For the Canadian experience not acceptable, but you may claim it for your outside Canada experience

If you have self-employed experience, you need to provide more documents to verify it. For example, consider the following.

- A reference letter from a credible third-party, such as an independent accountant or a lawyer
- Samples of your contracts with your clients
- Reference letters from your clients
- Reference letters from your suppliers or parallel businesses
- List of employees with their roles and contact information
- Reference letters from your employees (freelance, contract, part-time, full-time)
- Pictures of you at work
- Tax documents of your business
- Media articles that critique your work
- ….

It is quite common for the officers to ask for the skill level of your job under the Canadian National Occupational Classifications. Read Tip # 16 for more details.

TIP # 19: APPLICATION STATUS

Mojiz is an international student in Canada. He is originally from Morocco. Mojiz got married to Canadian citizen a few months ago. His spouse initiated the process of immigration to him under the inside Canada spousal sponsorship program. Mojiz is anxious to know the status of his application. He hasn't heard from the immigration authorities for the past two months.

There is no doubt the immigration application process is time-consuming. It sometimes takes months or even years for the Canadian immigration authorities at IRCC to review and finalize an application. One of the methods to view the status of your application is to visit the **eCAS** or rather the *electronic Client Application Status* page. Follow these steps to view the status of your application.

1. Visit the eCAS main page at https://services3.cic.gc.ca/ecas/security.do
2. Accept the terms and conditions
3. Enter your information.
    - You need to pick an identification type form the list. Most people pick the Application Number which is usually a single letter with some numbers following it (e.g. E123456789 for economic applications, V123456789 for visit visa or eTA applications,

F123456789 for family sponsorship applications, H123456789 for Humanitarian and Compassionate or rather H&C applications). Some application numbers begin with two letters such as economic applications under provincial nominee programs which begin with EP (e.g. EP12345678). You need to replace 123456789 with your actual application number. Do not miss the first letter.

- You may pick your UCI or Unique Client Identification number. A UCI consists of either eight digits or 10 digits. If you select and enter the UCI option, you could see all the applications under your name (e.g. a visit visa application and an immigration application).
- Make sure to enter your information correctly and based on the information you have provided to IRCC. Also, keep in mind that you could extract your file number or UCI from email correspondences you've received from them.

4. Explore the status of your application.

TROUBLESHOOTING

If you are not able to see the results, you may have entered the information incorrectly. Go back to the previous page and re-enter your info. Also, remember the data you enter needs to match the information IRCC has already shared with you. If the problem persists, you may have disabled access to your online status by mistake.

If the problem persists, you need to get in touch with IRCC and ask for help. You may contact IRCC via their Web Form at http://www.cic.gc.ca/english/contacts/web-form.asp or if you live in Canada contact their toll-free number 1-888-242-2100 (for hearing impaired call 1-888-576-8502). The phone number is not available outside Canada. It is also very difficult to get hold of them. That's why the web form is probably a better option.

The most reliable piece of information you receive from IRCC are the emails they send you directly. If you see discrepancies between the emails and the eCAS system, it is likely there is something wrong with the eCAS. However, to be on the safe side contact IRCC as soon as you can.

If you have an online account with IRCC, you may also see the status of your application there (e.g. the Express Entry applicants).

TIP # 20: REGISTER A BUSINESS IN CANADA

Erhi is a successful business owner in Mongolia. She intends to expand her business to Canada. The ultimate intention is to get a work permit. As part of the project, Erhi wants to register a corporation in the province of Manitoba. She wonders how to proceed.

Some immigration or work permit applicants need to start businesses in Canada before or upon their arrival. For example, consider the following options:

- Startup visa immigration to Canada (see Tip # 33)
- A work permit under LMIA exemption code C11 (see Tip # 35)

The current Tip explains what you potentially need to consider before registering a business.

TYPES OF BUSINESSES IN CANADA

Depending on the province of destination the business type you may register could vary, but generally speaking, these are the main business types in Canada:

- **Sole proprietorship** – You are the only owner and operator of the business. This is the simplest form of business. It is very easy to register, and it costs less to operate. There are also no chances of double-taxation as your personal and business tax is the same. However, you are fully liable for your business. If an entity sues the business, you are fully responsible for it, and you may lose your personal property to cover the lawsuit against your business. If a sole business goes bankrupt, then the owner will also go bankrupt.

- **Partnership** – Partnership is somewhat similar to a sole proprietorship, but instead of one owner, there are multiple owners. Each of the partners is fully liable for the business (depending on the province of the business, sometimes some of the owners could have limited liability). A partnership business usually takes shape between people who are very close and fully trust each other.

- **Incorporation** – An incorporated business is a separate entity from its owners, and that's why the owners' liabilities are limited to the business only (some exceptions apply). In Canada, a corporation may have one or more owners. The registration process of such businesses is more complex and costlier, and there is a chance of double-taxation because you pay the corporate taxes, and then on top of that, you pay personal taxes. There are some tax relief systems in place to mitigate it though.

The preceding definitions are very broad. Depending on the province of the destination and the owners (e.g. foreign nationals or a group of businesses), the structure of the business could differ. When it comes to immigration or work permit to Canada, the recommended option is incorporation. Sometimes the other two options are not even available to the applicant.

FEDERAL VS. PROVINCIAL

You may register your business provincially or federally. There is not much difference between these two options. In theory, if you register the business federally, you may operate in any province of Canada, and your name is protected everywhere in the country. However, this is not quite true. Many provinces expect federal corporations to make certain arrangements in their province to operate. The preferred option to visa and immigration applicants is federal registration, but you need to consult with a chartered accountant or a corporate lawyer to make up your mind.

RESIDENCY REQUIREMENTS FOR THE DIRECTORS

Canada is a member of the WTO (World Trade Organization). Our country is part of the free world of trades. We have signed many international trade agreements with other countries such as CETA and USMCA (formerly NAFTA). Consequently, Canada welcomes foreign nationals' investments. Regardless, some limitations exist over business registrations for them. A typical corporation has some shareholders and a board of directors. Shareholders are the owners of the company. They usually invest their own money in the business to make it happen. Some exceptions exist. For example, some shareholders do not invest in the business or do not have the right to vote.

The board of directors of a corporation is the governing body of the business. They are the policymakers of the business. They, for example, hire and fire the CEO (Chief Executive Officer) of the business and oversee her or his management. They also monitor the financial health of the business and more. A member of the board of directors is called a director of the business. Directors may or may not be shareholders. It is, however, customary for a director to be a shareholder.

Both the federal government and many Canadian provinces expect a certain percentage of directors of a company to be Canadian citizens or permanent residents of Canada. The following table shows the residency requirements for each province in Canada[11].

Jurisdiction	Directors' Residency Requirements
Federal (Canada)	Yes At least 25% of the directors of a corporation must be resident Canadians. However, if a corporation has less than four directors, at least one director must be a resident Canadian.
Alberta	Yes At least 25% of the directors of a corporation must be resident Canadians. However, if a corporation has less than four directors, at least one director must be a resident Canadian.
British-Columbia	No requirements

Jurisdiction	Directors' Residency Requirements
Prince Edward Island	No requirements
Ontario	Yes At least 25% of the directors of a corporation must be resident Canadians. However, if a corporation has less than four directors, at least one director must be a resident Canadian.
Manitoba	Yes At least 25% of the directors of a corporation must be resident Canadians. However, if a corporation has less than four directors, at least one director must be a resident Canadian.
New Brunswick	No requirements
Nova Scotia	No requirements
Nunavut	No requirements
Quebec	No requirements (Not in the actual Companies Act and not in the future new Business Corporations Act in Quebec).
Saskatchewan	Yes At least 25% of the directors of a corporation must be resident Canadians. However, if a corporation has less than four directors, at least one director must be a resident Canadian.

Jurisdiction	Directors' Residency Requirements
Newfoundland and Labrador	Yes At least 25% of the directors of a corporation must be resident Canadians. However, if a corporation has less than four directors, at least one director must be a resident Canadian.
Northwest Territories	No requirements
Yukon	No requirements

BUSINESS NAME

You may register your business without picking a name. We call these businesses "numbered companies." If you do not choose a name for your company, then a typical name for it will be, "123456 Ontario Inc.". If you decide to choose a name for your company, you need to make sure the name does not resemble other names to avoid future legal issues.

BUSINESS NAME EXTENSIONS

Having an extension for the business name is customary in Canada. Some extensions could be Ltd, Inc, and Corp. There is no legal difference between these extensions. You may pick anyone you like or do not pick anyone at all.

OTHER MATTERS TO CONSIDER

Corporations need a sales tax number to be able to collect sales taxes. Companies collect these taxes on behalf of the provincial and federal governments and will eventually return them to those governments. Depending on the province you are operating, sales tax is called GST, HST, PST, or other names. Read Tip # 88 for more details.

If you intend to hire people, then you also need to inform the Canada Revenue Agency (CRA) and other government entities. You also need to set up a payroll account with the CRA.

If your company intends to import or export goods, you need to inform the authorities. If this is not your initial intent, you may later inform them.

ASKING HELP FROM PROFESSIONALS

Due to the complexities of business registration, I highly recommend getting help from professionals. A corporate lawyer can help you set up the structure of your business. A professional accountant may also help you register the business. You may do all of these yourself, but I highly doubt it if this is a good idea.

---

[11] I received the residency of directors' table from my former accountant. I am not quite sure about the source of the information. That's why I haven't cited the source. When you are registering your business, make sure to double-check these requirements with your lawyer or accountant.

PART TWO: IMMIGRATION TO CANADA

TIP # 21: ECONOMIC IMMIGRATION

Annalena is a business analyst from Liechtenstein. She holds a bachelor's degree in economics. Annalena has been working for a business consulting firm for the past ten years. She is 32 years old. Annalena speaks German, English, and French languages fluently. Her net worth is $600,000. Annalena is wondering if she could move to Canada permanently. She has heard about economic immigration to Canada but has no idea what this phrase means.

Canada offers three routes for immigration, namely:

- **Family reunification** for people who are sponsored by their family members to Canada (practitioners see subsection 12(1) of IRPA)

- **Economic immigration** for applicants who may economically establish themselves in Canada without the use of social assistance program (practitioners see subsection 12(2) of IRPA)

- **Refugees** for convention refugees and those who need protection (practitioners see subsection 12(3) of IRPA)

Majority of immigrants move to Canada under the economic immigration programs. We may divide these immigrants into the following major groups.

- Federal economic immigrants
- Quebec-selected skilled workers and business
- Provincial or territorial nominees

FEDERAL ECONOMIC IMMIGRANTS

Federal options are for those who intend to settle anywhere in Canada but Quebec. The subcategories of federal economic immigration methods include:

- **Express Entry** – This is an online system of applying for immigration to Canada that covers three streams of immigration:
    - *Federal Skilled Worker Program* – An immigration option for those who apply based on their education, work experience, knowledge of English or French languages, age, job opportunities in Canada, and adaptability to our country (see Tip # 23 and 24).
    - *Canadian Experience Class* – If you have recently worked in Canada for at least one year, you could qualify for this option. This option is the most popular Express Entry option for those who have already entered Canada with a valid work permit or in some cases a study permit (see Tip # 25).
    - *Federal Skilled Trades Program* – This method encourages skilled tradespeople to immigrate to Canada. There is a limited list of acceptable jobs (see Tip # 26).
- **Federal Self-employed Class** – Despite its generic name, this method is limited to self-employed people under the following categories only (see Tip # 30).
    - *Self-employed people in cultural activities* – Traditionally covers performing artists, visual artists, authors, experts in fine arts, etc. (see Tip # 32).
    - *Self-employed people in athletics* – This option is for professional athletes, internationally acclaimed athletes, and coaches (see Tip # 31).
- **Start-up Visa** – If you have an innovative idea and receive support from certain organizations in Canada, you may

immigrate to Canada under this program (see Tip # 33).

- **Atlantic Immigration Pilot** – If you receive a valid job offer from an employer located in New Brunswick, Nova Scotia, Prince Edward Island, or Newfoundland and Labrador, you may immigrate to Canada. Since this is a pilot program, the government may stop it at any time.
- **Caregivers** – If you have worked as a caregiver for minor children or people with high medical needs, you may later apply for permanent residency under this program. The applicants usually work for two years or more with a valid work permit and then eventually file for permanent residency.

You may like to know, IRCC regularly reviews these options and they may add more options, remove some of the existing ones, or make changes to them.

QUEBEC-SELECTED SKILLED WORKERS AND BUSINESS

Quebec has a broad agreement with the federal government of Canada. Under this agreement, also known as Canada–Québec Accord, the government of Quebec has a high level of freedom regarding immigration to their province. Quebec is mostly interested in the immigration of Francophone (French-speaking) individuals.

PROVINCIAL/TERRITORIAL NOMINEES

Under section 95 of the Canadian Constitution Act 1867, provinces may pass and implement laws to select and control the influx of immigrants to their province. All Canadian provinces and territories except for Nunavut have special programs for immigration to their province. A typical *Provincial Nominee Program (PNP)* consists of two stages.

- Selection by the province or territory and receiving a Certificate of Nomination
- Approval by the federal government and securing the permanent residency

The federal government looks into two significant areas before issuing the permanent residency: The ability of the applicant to economically establish themselves in Canada and their admissibility to our country.

TIP # 22: EXPRESS ENTRY IMMIGRATION TO CANADA

Zaher is a citizen of Yemen. He holds a Ph.D. in biology. Zaher has been a university professor for the past ten years. He knows both the English and French languages well. Zaher is 39 years old. He is married with two children. Zaher's wife is 33. She knows English well, but she is not familiar with the French language. Zaher and his family want to immigration to Canada. They want to immigrate under the Express Entry system.

The largest group of immigrants to Canada are Economic Immigrants. For example, the 2017 Annual Report to Parliament on Immigration shows our country accepted 296,346 new immigrants in 2016, out of which 155,994 or rather 53% where Economic Immigrants.

NOTE: The destination of federal immigration is any province or territory of Canada, but Quebec. If you intend to immigrate to Quebec (e.g. to Montreal or Quebec City), you need to use one of the Quebec immigration options.

Economic Immigrants are further divided into several subcategories, namely:

- Federal Economic – Skilled (59,999 admitted in 2016)

- Federal Economic – Caregivers (18,467 admitted in 2016)
- Federal Economic – Business (867 admitted in 2016)
- Provincial Nominee (46,170 admitted in 2016)
- Quebec Skilled Workers (25,857 admitted in 2016)
- Quebec Business Immigrants (4,634 admitted in 2016)

All the statistics are taken from the Minister's 2017 Report to the Parliament.

The first and largest subcategory consists of the following three streams of immigration to Canada.

- The Federal Skilled Worker Program (FSWP) – Applicants in this group are normally young, highly educated, have some work experience in a professional capacity, and know English or French languages well (see Tips # 23 and 24).
- The Canadian Experience Class (CEC) – Applicants in this group normally have at least one year of full-time work experience in Canada in a professional capacity (see Tip # 25).
- The Federal Skilled Trades Program (FSTP) – Applicants in this group are normally licensed plumbers, welders, etc. (see Tip # 26).

The Government of Canada presented a system of immigration to Canada in 2015 to manage all applications under the FSWP, CEC, and FSTP programs. The name of this system is Express Entry or EE. Here is how EE works.

1. The applicant creates an online account on the IRCC website (Note: If the applicant hires a licensed representative, they create an account for the applicant on their special portal with IRCC).

2. The applicant enters basic information about their work experience, education, knowledge of the official languages of Canada, age, etc.

3. IRCC reviews the application. If it meets the conditions under any of the FSWP, CEC, or FSTP programs, the applicant enters the pool of Express Entry for up to one year. IRCC also calculates the points of the applicant under the Express Entry criteria. This pointing system is the Comprehensive Ranking System (CRS). Currently, a Candidate may receive up to 1200 points under the CRS system.

4. IRCC picks several applicants from the pool of Express Entry every few weeks. The rounds of selection happen a few times a year (usually at least once a month). Only those who hold the highest CRS scores will be invited to apply for immigration to Canada.

5. The invited applicant fills out a new set of forms and uploads several documents to the IRCC account to support their claims.

6. IRCC officers review those documents. If they are convinced the applicant is eligible, they ask the applicant to complete a medical examination via an approved physician, also known as the Panel Physician. They also complete background assessments and security screening to make sure the applicant is admissible to Canada.

7. If the applicant passes all the tests, they could land in Canada as a Permanent Resident.

Of course, the devil is in the details. I highly recommend studying this system carefully or consult with a licensed professional before initiating the application process. I have seen many people who applied on their own, but IRCC refused them for simple preventable mistakes.

TIP # 23: THE MINIMUM REQUIREMENTS FOR THE FEDERAL SKILLED WORKER PROGRAM

Sophia is a citizen of San Marino. She is a well educated professional with extensive work experience. Sophia intends to immigration to Canada as a skilled worker, but she doesn't know if she meets the minimum requirements for immigration to Canada.

The Federal Skilled Worker Program (FSWP or FSW) is one of the immigration options to Canada under the Express Entry system. FSWP targets people who may economically establish themselves in Canada because of their job experience, knowledge of English or French languages, age, education, and their adaptability to Canada. To apply under this program, you need to meet the minimum requirements and receive at least 67 points out of the existing 100 points allocated to this program.

The following table shows the minimum requirements to apply under the Federal Skilled Worker Program. If you do not meet these requirements, you will face refusal right after applying.

Qualifications	Minimum Requirements
Work Experience	- You need to mention an occupation as your main job - You need to show that in the past ten years from the time you submit your application you had at least one year of continuous full-time experience in that occupation. If you worked part-time, then you need to show that your experience was continuous and equal to at least one year of full-time experience. Full-time job means at least 30 hours of work per week. If you worked 15 hours per week, then you need to show two years of continuous job experience. If you worked 30 hours or more per week, then you need to show at least one year of experience. - Your main occupation needs to be a Skill Type 0 or Skill Level A or B under the Canadian National Occupational Classifications (NOC). Skill Type 0 covers management jobs. Skill Level A or B jobs are those that usually require a university degree or a post-secondary diploma (college education). See Tip # 16 for more information about NOC.
Language Skills	- Canada has two official languages: French and English. You need to know at least one of them. If you are familiar with both, then one of them becomes your first official language and the other one the second official language. You pick the one that you know better. - You must take an official language test. If you don't take any tests, IRCC will refuse your application immediately. - For the French language, you need to take either the TEF Canada or the TCF Canada tests - For the English language, you also have two options: CELPIP General and IELTS General - Not taking a test for the second language does not

Qualifications	Minimum Requirements
	result in refusal of your application, but you won't receive any points • If French is your first language and you are taking the TEF Canada test, you need to receive these minimum points to be able to apply: speaking (expression orale) – 310, listening (compréhension de l'orale) – 249, reading (compréhension de l'écrit) – 207, writing (expression écrite) – 310 • If French is your first language and you are taking the TCF Canada test, you need to receive these minimum points to be able to apply: speaking (expression orale) –10, listening (compréhension de l'orale) – 458, reading (compréhension de l'écrit) – 453, writing (expression écrite) – 10 • If English is your first language and you are taking the CELPIP General test, then you need to receive a score of 7 or more under every ability (i.e. speaking, listening, reading, and writing) • If English is your first language and you are taking the IELTS General test, then you need to receive a score of 6.0 or more under every ability (i.e. speaking, listening, reading, and writing) • IRCC does not accept other test results such as IELTS Academic, CELPIP General-LS, TOEFL, or DLF
Education	• If you have studied in Canada, you need to submit your official results (e.g. your bachelor's degree and transcript from an accredited Canadian university) • If you have studied outside Canada, you need to ask a designated assessment organization to evaluate your education credentials and finds the equivalency with the Canadian system. IRCC calls this process the Educational Credential Assessment (ECA). IRCC has currently approved the following entities: 　　o Comparative Education Service: University of

Qualifications	Minimum Requirements
	Toronto School of Continuing Studies ○ International Credential Assessment Service of Canada ○ World Education Services ○ International Qualifications Assessment Service ○ International Credential Evaluation Service • If you fail to show your educational credentials (i.e. either your Canadian or foreign credentials), IRCC will refuse your application promptly after submission.

Subsection 75(2) of the Immigration and Refugee Protection Regulations (IRPR) outlines these requirements. Do not apply if you do not meet the minimum requirements as the immigration officer will refuse your application immediately under subsection 75(3) of IRPR. Make sure to receive your ECA and take a language test before opening an Express Entry profile. Also, contact your employer(s) and get reference letters, employment contracts, etc. to make sure you meet the work experience requirements.

Do not forget that on top of the minimum requirements you need to receive at least 67 out of 100 points to be eligible under the Federal Skilled Worker Program. See Tip # 24 for the FSWP point system.

Depending on whether you have a valid job offer to Canada or not, you may also need to show that you have access to some settlement funds. A 6-month LICO defines the minimum threshold for the settlement funds. See Tip # 29 to know more about LICO.

FEDERAL SKILLED WORKER PROGRAM AND EXPRESS ENTRY

The Federal Skilled Worker Program has been a subcategory of the Express Entry system since January 2015. See Tip # 22 for more information on Express Entry.

TIP # 24: FEDERAL SKILLED WORKER PROGRAM – POINT SYSTEM

Mateo is a Colombian architect. He holds a master's degree from an American accredited university. He knows English very well. Mateo is 48 years old. He is married to his wife, Luciana. His wife holds a bachelor's degree in graphic design. Luciana's sister, who is a Canadian citizen, lives in Ottawa, Ontario. Mateo has worked full-time for a well-respected Colombian construction company in the past ten years. He wonders if he qualifies for immigration to Canada. He is especially concerned about his age.

If you are applying for immigration to Canada as a Federal Skilled Worker Program (FSWP) candidate, you need to meet both the minimum requirements and the minimum necessary points. Read Tip # 23 for more information about the minimum requirements of FSWP.

The minimum points are 67 out of 100 possible points. You may like to know; these points cover six factors:

1. Knowledge of official Canadian languages (i.e. English and French) – up to 28 points
2. Education credentials – up to 25 points

3. Work experience – up to 15 points
4. Age of the principal applicant – up to 12 points
5. A valid job-offer in Canada (arranged employment) – up to 10 points
6. Adaptability – up to 10 points

KNOWLEDGE OF CANADIAN OFFICIAL LANGUAGES

Canada has two official languages; French and English. You need to be familiar with at least one of them. You also need to take an acceptable language test to prove your ability to an immigration officer. Consider the following:

- If you know one official language, you will receive a maximum of 24 points.
- For the second official language, you could receive up to 4 more points.
- The points are based on each of the four language abilities (i.e. speaking, listening, reading, and writing). The overall score of the test is not important.
- The only approved English tests are CELPIP and IELTS General
- The only approved French tests are TEF Canada and TCF Canada
- IRCC may change the approved tests and scoring system from time to time

EDUCATION CREDENTIALS

If you completed your education outside Canada, you need to provide an acceptable Educational Credential Assessment (ECA) report to the IRCC. The maximum points for education are 25. See Tip # 23 for a list of ECA organizations.

WORK EXPERIENCE

The following list shows the breakdown of points for work experience. Your experience needs to be equivalent to a full-time job in the past ten years. Only work experience in a NOC 0, A, or B job is acceptable. See Tip # 16 for information about the NOC system.

- Six years or more – 15 points
- Four to five years – 13 points
- Two to three years – 11 points
- One year – 9 points
- Under one year – 0 points and the refusal of the application.

AGE OF THE PRINCIPAL APPLICANT

You may receive up to 12 points for age, based on the following table.

Age	Points
18-35	12
36	11
37	10
38	9
39	8
40	7
41	6
42	5
43	4
44	3
45	2
46	1
Under 18	0
47 and older	0

A VALID JOB OFFER IN CANADA (ARRANGED EMPLOYMENT)

As a general rule, the job offer needs the backup of an LMIA. A valid job offer needs to meet the following:

- A NOC 0, A, or B job
- A full-time job for at least one year
- You can do the job and if necessary, get all the required licenses in Canada

If you receive a valid job offer, you will be exempt from the minimum settlement funds. You also receive 10 points. See Tip # 49 for information on LMIA and Tip # 28 for job offer requirements.

ADAPTABILITY

Adaptability offers you a maximum of 10 points. You may receive points under the following subcategories. PA refers to the Principal Applicant in the following list.

- PA's spouse or partner's language level (the equivalent of CLB 4 or higher) – 5 points
- PA's past studies in Canada (at least two years of full-time secondary or post-secondary studies) – 5 points
- PA's spouse or partner's past studies in Canada (at least two years of full-time secondary or post-secondary studies) – 5 points
- PA's past work experience in Canada (at least one-year full time in NOC type 0 or level A or B with a valid work permit) – 5 points
- PA's spouse or common-law partner's past work experience in Canada – 5 points
- PA's valid job offer to Canada (arranged employment) – 5 points (on top of the ten independent points you receive because of this job offer)
- Relatives in Canada (either the PA or the spouse or common-law partner of the PA) – 5 points

Relatives must currently be living in Canada. They have to be Canadian citizens or permanent residents. They also need to be at least 18 years old.

Acceptable relatives include the following regarding the PA or the PA's spouse or common-law partner:

- children or grandchildren
- parents or grandparents
- siblings (brothers or sisters)
- nephews or nieces
- uncles or aunts (by marriage or blood)

FEDERAL SKILLED WORKER PROGRAM AND EXPRESS ENTRY

The Federal Skilled Worker Program has been a subcategory of the Express Entry system since January 2015. See Tip # 22 for more information on Express Entry.

TIP # 25: CANADIAN EXPERIENCE CLASS

Sofia, a Spanish citizen, is 24 years old. She entered Canada as an international student when she was 19. Sonia completed a four-year bachelor's program at the University of Saskatchewan. She then received a job offer from an employer in Vancouver. It is now about 14 months since she has been working for her Canadian employer as a Marketing Analyst on a full-time basis. Sonia took a CELPIP test a few months ago. She intends to immigrate to Canada, but she wonders what the best option for her will be, considering she does not have significant funds in her bank account.

One of the options to immigrate to Canada is the Canadian Experience Class (CEC) program. CEC is a suitable option for some of the people who have work experience in Canada.

MINIMUM WORK EXPERIENCE REQUIREMENTS

Acceptable work experience must meet the following requirements:

- It occurred in the past three years, and
- it happened in Canada, and
- it was at least one year of full-time experience equivalent, and
- it wasn't a self-employed job, and
- it was under skill levels 0, A, or B.

Read the following Tips for more information about work experience and skill levels.

- Tip # 18: Definition of Full-time Work Experience
- Tip # 16: National Occupational Classification (NOC)

ACCEPTABLE LANGUAGE TESTS

You need to take at least one of the following tests.

- **CELPIP**: Canadian English Language Proficiency Index Program (Only CELPIP General is acceptable. Don't take General-LS)
- **IELTS**: International English Language Testing System (Only IELTS General is acceptable. Don't take the IELTS Academic)
- **TEF Canada**: Test d'évaluation de français
- **TCF Canada**: Test de connaissance du français

You only need to take one of the tests per language. If you present multiple test results under the same language, the officer considers the latest test results. They won't combine the results. While taking the second language test is not mandatory, it could enhance your Express Entry CRS score significantly.

MINIMUM LANGUAGE REQUIREMENTS IF YOUR JOB IS SKILL LEVELS 0 AND A

You need to take an official language test (either English or French) and meet the minimum requirements below for skill levels 0 or A.

Test	Language	Speaking	Listening	Reading	Writing
CELPIP	English	7	7	7	7
IELTS General	English	6.0	6.0	6.0	6.0
TEF Canada	French	310	249	207	310
TCF Canada	French	10	458	453	10

The figures above are minimums. You need to meet the minimum under each ability (i.e. speaking, listening, reading, and writing). Even if your score falls under the minimum for one of the abilities, you may not apply. Since you will eventually compete with other Express Entry applicants, you need to get much better scores than these minimums.

MINIMUM LANGUAGE REQUIREMENTS IF YOUR JOB IS SKILL LEVEL B

You need to take an official language test (either English or French) and meet the minimum requirements below for skill level B.

Test	Language	Speaking	Listening	Reading	Writing
CELPIP	English	5	5	5	5
IELTS General	English	5.0	5.0	4.0	5.0
TEF Canada	French	226	181	151	226
TCF Canada	French	6	369	375	6

The figures above are minimums. You need to meet the minimum under each ability (i.e. speaking, listening, reading, and writing). Even if your score falls under the minimum for one of the abilities, you may not apply. Since you will eventually compete with other Express Entry applicants, you need to get much better scores than these minimums.

OTHER REQUIREMENTS

Although there are no other minimum requirements for CEC, the following factors affect your Express Entry CRS score:

- Age
- Education
- Work experience outside Canada
- Spouse or common-law partner's education and knowledge of official languages
- Sisters or brothers who are Canadian citizens or permanent residents and live in Canada
- ….

EXEMPTION FROM SETTLEMENT FUNDS

When you apply under CEC, you do not need to show settlement funds (i.e. a minimum amount of money in your bank account). However, I highly recommend you hold at least equivalent to LICO in your bank account. See Tip # 29 for more details on LICO.

CANADIAN EXPERIENCE CLASS & EXPRESS ENTRY

The Canadian Experience Class is a subcategory of the Express Entry system since January 2015. Read Tip # 22 for more details.

TIP # 26: FEDERAL SKILLED TRADES PROGRAM

Alessandra is a Peruvian citizen. She is 27 years old. Alessandra is a carpenter supervisor. She learned carpentry when she was 20 years old. She then started working as a professional carpenter at the age of 21. Alessandra gradually climbed the ladder and became a supervisor at the age of 24. She knows the English language well. She took the IELTS General test last month, and her score was 7.0 under all the abilities. Alessandra has recently received a job offer from a large carpentry firm in Nova Scotia, Canada. They have already received a positive LMIA to hire Alessandra. She wonders if she could immigrate to Canada.

The most popular method of immigration to Canada is the Express Entry system. As I have explained in other Tips, this system covers the following immigration options.

- Federal Skilled Worker Program (FSWP)
- Canadian Experience Class (CEC)
- Federal Skilled Trades Program (FSTP)

The last option is the focus of this Tip. If your job falls under any acceptable FSTP categories, you'd probably need to consider this option for your immigration to Canada. To learn more about acceptable job categories, read Tip # 27.

MINIMUM WORK EXPERIENCE FOR FSTP

You need to show that within the last five years you have had at least two years of work experience under any of the acceptable skilled trade jobs. The work experience needs to be either full-time or equivalent to full-time. You also need to show your job duties matches the job duties an immigration officer expects under the job category you apply.

MINIMUM LANGUAGE REQUIREMENTS FOR FSTP

You need to take at least one of the following tests.

- **CELPIP**: Canadian English Language Proficiency Index Program (Only CELPIP General is acceptable. Don't take General-LS)
- **IELTS**: International English Language Testing System (Only IELTS General is acceptable. Don't take IELTS Academic)
- **TEF Canada**: Test d'évaluation de français
- **TCF Canada**: Test de connaissance du français

You only need to take one of the tests per language. If you present multiple test results under the same language, the officer considers the latest test results. They won't combine the results. While taking the second language test is not mandatory, it could enhance your Express Entry CRS score significantly.

The following table shows the minimum scores under each ability of the test for the FSTP applicants.

The figures below are minimums. You need to meet the minimum under each ability (i.e. speaking, listening, reading, and writing). Even if your score falls under the minimum for one of the abilities, you may not apply. Since you will eventually compete with other Express Entry applicants, you need to get much better scores than these minimums.

Test	Language	Speaking	Listening	Reading	Writing
CELPIP	English	5	5	4	4
IELTS General	English	5.0	5.0	3.5	4.0
TEF Canada	French	226	181	121	181
TCF Canada	French	6	369	342	4

JOB OFFER OR CERTIFICATE OF QUALIFICATIONS

You may only apply under the FSTP if you have either of these:

- A valid job offer under any of the FSTP job categories from a Canadian employer, or
- A certificate of qualification issued by Canadian federal, provincial, or territorial authority

The job offer could be from one or two Canadian employers. There are many other conditions attached to a valid job offer (see Tip # 28)

Certain government bodies issue certificates of qualification for skilled trade jobs. Visit the following links for each province. Quebec is missing from this list as Express Entry immigration is for anywhere in Canada but the province of Quebec.

Provinces (from west to east):

- **British Columbia** – settler.ca/88/fstp/bc
- **Alberta** – settler.ca/88/fstp/ab
- **Saskatchewan** – settler.ca/88/fstp/sk
- **Manitoba** – settler.ca/88/fstp/mb
- **Ontario** – settler.ca/88/fstp/on
- **New Brunswick** – settler.ca/88/fstp/nb

- **Nova Scotia** – settler.ca/88/fstp/ns
- **Prince Edward Island** – settler.ca/88/fstp/pe
- **Newfoundland and Labrador** – settler.ca/88/fstp/nl

Territories (from west to east):

- **Yukon** – settler.ca/88/fstp/yt
- **Northwest Territories** – settler.ca/88/fstp/nt
- **Nunavut** – settler.ca/88/fstp/nu

Canadian provinces or territories do not regulate some skilled trades. You may visit the following website to see your potential alternative options for those jobs.

- The Canadian Information Centre for International Credentials – settler.ca/88/fstp/ic

Since the actual websites could change at any time and also the URLs are usually very lengthy; I have created shortcuts to them. So the addresses you see above are short URLs, not the actual websites.

OTHER REQUIREMENTS

Although there no other minimum requirements for FSTP (Federal Skilled Trades Program), the following factors affect your Express Entry CRS score:

- Age
- Education
- Work experience outside Canada
- Spouse or common-law partner's education and knowledge of official languages
- Sisters or brothers who are Canadian citizens or permanent residents and live in Canada
- ….

Majority of FSTP applicants do not receive enough CRS score. Therefore, they are not able to compete with the CEC and FSWP applicants. That's why the government of Canada usually runs special rounds of invitation (ITA) for the FSTP applicants twice a year. So if your points are not good enough, don't get disappointed. You could have a chance within the next six months or so.

EXEMPTION FROM SETTLEMENT FUNDS

When you apply under FSTP (Federal Skilled Trades Program), you need to show settlement funds (i.e. a minimum amount of money in your bank account). See Tip # 29 for more information on settlement funds.

If you have a valid work permit along with a valid job offer, you are exempt from showing settlement funds. Despite that, I highly recommend following Tip # 29 guidelines to avoid any potential issues with the immigration authorities.

FEDERAL SKILLED TRADES PROGRAM (FSTP) & EXPRESS ENTRY

FSTP is a subgroup of the Express Entry system since January 2015. See Tip # 22 for more details on this system.

TIP # 27: LIST OF JOBS FOR THE FEDERAL SKILLED TRADES PROGRAM

Yul is a 27-year-old millwright from Mongolia. He holds a post-secondary diploma from a technical college in his hometown Ulaanbaatar. Yul has more than five years of full-time work experience in his field. He wonders if he can immigrate to Canada under the FSTP program.

If you are applying to immigrate to Canada under the Federal Skilled Trades Program (FSTP) your work experience needs to fall under one of the following classifications. Before reviewing the list consider the following:

- If you are not familiar with NOC codes, see Tip # 16
- For more information about the FSTP program, see Tip # 26

You also may refer to the following link to check out the lead statement and main duties of each NOC code. Your job must match the lead statement and most of the main duties mentioned under each code.

settler.ca/88/noc

MAJOR GROUP 72, INDUSTRIAL, ELECTRICAL AND CONSTRUCTION TRADES

NOC Code	NOC Title
7201	Contractors and supervisors, machining, metal forming, shaping and erecting trades and related occupations
7202	Contractors and supervisors, electrical trades and telecommunications occupations
7203	Contractors and supervisors, pipefitting trades
7204	Contractors and supervisors, carpentry trades
7205	Contractors and supervisors, other construction trades, installers, repairers and servicers
7231	Machinists and machining and tooling inspectors
7232	Tool and die makers
7233	Sheet metal workers
7234	Boilermakers
7235	Structural metal and platework fabricators and fitters
7236	Ironworkers
7237	Welders and related machine operators
7241	Electricians (except industrial and power system)
7242	Industrial electricians
7243	Power system electricians
7244	Electrical power line and cable workers
7245	Telecommunications line and cable workers
7246	Telecommunications installation and repair workers
7247	Cable television service and maintenance technicians
7251	Plumbers
7252	Steamfitters, pipefitters and sprinkler system installers
7253	Gas fitters

NOC Code	NOC Title
7271	Carpenters
7272	Cabinetmakers
7281	Bricklayers
7282	Concrete finishers
7283	Tilesetters
7284	Plasterers, drywall installers and finishers and lathers
7291	Roofers and shinglers
7292	Glaziers
7293	Insulators
7294	Painters and decorators (except interior decorators)
7295	Floor covering installers

MAJOR GROUP 73, MAINTENANCE AND EQUIPMENT OPERATION TRADES

NOC Code	NOC Title
7301	Contractors and supervisors, mechanic trades
7302	Contractors and supervisors, heavy equipment operator crews
7303	Supervisors, printing and related occupations
7304	Supervisors, railway transport operations
7305	Supervisors, motor transport and other ground transit operators
7311	Construction millwrights and industrial mechanics
7312	Heavy-duty equipment mechanics
7313	Heating, refrigeration and air conditioning mechanics
7314	Railway carmen/women
7315	Aircraft mechanics and aircraft inspectors

NOC Code	NOC Title
7316	Machine fitters
7318	Elevator constructors and mechanics
7321	Automotive service technicians, truck and bus mechanics and mechanical repairers
7322	Motor vehicle body repairers
7331	Oil and solid fuel heating mechanics
7332	Appliance servicers and repairers
7333	Electrical mechanics
7334	Motorcycle, all-terrain vehicle and other related mechanics
7335	Other small engine and small equipment repairers
7361	Railway and yard locomotive engineers
7362	Railway conductors and brakemen/women
7371	Crane operators
7372	Drillers and blasters - surface mining, quarrying and construction
7373	Water well drillers
7381	Printing press operators
7384	Other trades and related occupations, n.e.c.

MAJOR GROUP 82, SUPERVISORS AND TECHNICAL JOBS IN NATURAL RESOURCES, AGRICULTURE AND RELATED PRODUCTION

NOC Code	NOC Title
8211	Supervisors, logging and forestry
8221	Supervisors, mining and quarrying
8222	Contractors and supervisors, oil and gas drilling and services

NOC Code	NOC Title
8231	Underground production and development miners
8232	Oil and gas well drillers, servicers, testers and related workers
8241	Logging machinery operators
8252	Agricultural service contractors, farm supervisors and specialized livestock workers
8255	Contractors and supervisors, landscaping, grounds maintenance and horticulture services
8261	Fishing masters and officers
8262	Fishermen/women

MAJOR GROUP 92, PROCESSING, MANUFACTURING AND UTILITIES SUPERVISORS AND CENTRAL CONTROL OPERATORS

NOC Code	NOC Title
9211	Supervisors, mineral and metal processing
9212	Supervisors, petroleum, gas and chemical processing and utilities
9213	Supervisors, food and beverage processing
9214	Supervisors, plastic and rubber products manufacturing
9215	Supervisors, forest products processing
9217	Supervisors, textile, fabric, fur and leather products processing and manufacturing
9221	Supervisors, motor vehicle assembling
9222	Supervisors, electronics manufacturing
9223	Supervisors, electrical products manufacturing
9224	Supervisors, furniture and fixtures manufacturing

NOC Code	NOC Title
9226	Supervisors, other mechanical and metal products manufacturing
9227	Supervisors, other products manufacturing and assembly
9231	Central control and process operators, mineral and metal processing
9232	Central control and process operators, petroleum, gas and chemical processing
9235	Pulping, papermaking and coating control operators
9241	Power engineers and power systems operators
9243	Water and waste treatment plant operators

MINOR GROUP 632, CHEFS AND COOKS

NOC Code	NOC Title
6321	Chefs
6322	Cooks

MINOR GROUP 633, BUTCHERS AND BAKERS

NOC Code	NOC Title
6331	Butchers, meat cutters and fishmongers – retail and wholesale
6332	Bakers

Simply falling under one of these job categories do not qualify you to apply. Read Tip # 26 for all the requirements of this immigration option.

TIP # 28: JOB OFFER FOR EXPRESS ENTRY

Min Jun is a Korean citizen. He is 32 years old. Min Jun entered Canada as an international student for more than two years ago. He completed his MBA in Edmonton, Alberta. He then started working for a financial firm in Regina, Saskatchewan. Min Jun has now more than one year of full-time work experience in Canada. He intends to apply for permanent residency under the Express Entry system. Min Jun knows if he receives a job offer from an employer, he could enhance his chances of success. He wonders what needs to be included in the job offer.

A valid job offer, also known as an offer of employment or an arranged employment offer (AEO), could significantly enhance your chances to immigrate to Canada under the Express Entry system. You need to know, the specifications of the job offer depend on the subcategory of Express Entry you are applying. Just as a quick reminder, the subcategories of Express Entry are the following:

- Federal Skilled Worker Program (FSWP) – Tip # 23 & 24
- Canadian Experience Class (CEC) – Tip # 25
- Federal Skilled Trades Program (FSTP) – Tip # 26 & 27

JOB OFFER FOR FSWP AND CEC

A job offer for FSWP or CEC needs to meet the following criteria:

- Be valid for at least one year from the time you become a permanent resident of Canada
- Be full-time or rather at least 30 hours per week
- Be paid and continuous
- Be issued by one employer only
- Falls under NOC 0, A, or B

IRCC does not accept seasonal, self-employed, or contract-basis jobs.

JOB OFFER FOR FSTP

A job offer for FSTP needs to meet the following criteria:

- Be valid for at least one year from the time you become a permanent resident of Canada
- Be full-time or rather at least 30 hours per week
- Be paid and continuous
- Be issued by less than three employers
- Falls under acceptable jobs for FSTP (see Tip # 27)

IRCC does not accept seasonal, self-employed, or contract-basis jobs. Part-time jobs are acceptable only if you receive valid offers from two employers and the combination of two offers is equivalent to a full-time job. For example, you will work 10 hours per week for the first employer and 20 hours per week for the second one.

LMIA AND JOB OFFERS

Generally speaking, a job offer needs to be backed by a positive permanent residency LMIA (Labour Market Impact Assessment). However, your employer may not need a permanent residency LMIA if either of the following scenarios applies to you.

- You are currently working for the employer with a valid work permit backed by an LMIA. Your work permit is valid at the time of applying under Express Entry and remains valid till they finalize the application. For CEC and FSWP applicants, the NOC must be 0, A, or B. For FSTP applicants; the job must be the same job that you mention on your permanent residency application.

- You are currently working for the employer with a valid work permit that is exempt from an LMIA. You have at least one year of full-time work experience in Canada with the same employer and the same LMIA-exempt job.

A simple work permit is not good enough. For example, you may not apply because you hold a valid post-graduate work permit (PGWP) or an open work permit because of your spouse. Your work permit needs to be an employer-based work permit. You also need to meet the rest of the requirements I present in this Tip.

THE CONTENT OF THE JOB OFFER LETTER

When you submit your application, you need to show a job offer letter from your employer. The job offer letter must include the following:

- Start date of the job and validity of it. For example, it clearly says the job offer is valid for at least one year from the day you become a permanent resident of Canada. It may also be an indefinite job offer (or rather no expiry date)

- The name and contact information of the employer (address, website, email, phone numbers, etc.)

- LMIA number, if applicable. If the job is exempt from an LMIA, present the existing work permit with at least one supporting document.

- NOC code of the job

- The job title and duties

- The salary, hours of work, benefits, deductions, etc.

IRCC does not accept job offers from a high commission, an embassy, or a consulate in Canada.

Just because you are working for an employer in Canada, does not mean you have a job offer. You need to receive the job offer in writing with the specifications I have indicated in this Tip.

TIP # 29: LOW-INCOME CUT-OFF TABLE (LICO)

Elijah is an Israeli citizen. He is a 27-year-old mechanical engineer in the field of mechanical design. Elijah completed his Master's degree three years ago. He then started working for a manufacturing firm as a maintenance engineer. Elijah is married and has a six-month-old daughter. Both Elijah and his wife know English and French languages very well. They intend to immigrate to Canada under the Express Entry system. He has heard he needs to show proof of funds when he immigrates to Canada. Someone told him the settlement funds he shows need to match the LICO table. He wonders what LICO is and how he can prove the settlement funds.

Immigrants to Canada need to show they intend to live in our country independently and without using social assistance. There are many ways to confirm you want to be an independent newcomer to Canada. For example, an immigration officer may consider your skills, work experience, educational credentials, and your assets.

One of the options to prove your ability to be independent is the settlement funds. If you wonder, settlement funds refer to the amount of money you can bring to Canada when you land as a newcomer. Immigration authorities use the LICO table as a tool to evaluate the sufficiency of settlement funds.

WHAT IS LICO?

Low-income Cut-off (LICO) table represents the poverty line in urban areas of Canada with a population of 500,000 or more. In other words, if your income is below LICO, you are poor. LICO changes every year due to inflation. The following table shows LICO for those people who intend to immigrate to Canada in 2019. Your settlement funds need to be equal to or higher than the values of this table based on your family size. Please note that this table is not valid for parental sponsorship. If you need to know the minimum necessary income for parental sponsorship, read Tip # 42.

LICO TABLE 2019

Size of Family Unit	LICO – 12 Months	LICO – 6 Months
1 person	$25,338	$12,669
2 persons	$31,544	$15,772
3 persons	$38,780	$19,390
4 persons	$47,084	$23,542
5 persons	$53,402	$26,701
6 persons	$60,228	$30,114
7 persons	$67,056	$33,528
If more than 7 persons, for each additional person, add	$6,828	$3,414

Since these figures change year over year visit the following link for the latest LICO table.

settler.ca/88/lico

Most immigration options like the Federal Skilled Worker Program require proof of funds based on a 6-month LICO. Keep in mind, I have done my best to show the correct figures, but the numbers I have presented here are not the official numbers. Consequently, consult with other sources as well.

Note that funds need to be unencumbered, meaning you can easily have access to them. No strings attached! Consult with your immigration representative or the IRCC website for how you could prove you have access to these funds.

TIP # 30: FEDERAL SELF-EMPLOYED PROGRAM

Jelena is a 22-year-old professional swimmer from Montenegro. She has competed at the Olympics and two world championship cups in the past five years. Jelena holds several local, national, regional, and world medals. She intends to immigrate to Canada, but wonders if this is even possible.

Canada welcomes tens of thousands of immigrants every year. A large group of those people immigrate to Canada under the Federal programs. These programs target the individuals who want to live in any province or territory of Canada, but Quebec. Some of these immigrants are self-employed people. The Federal Government of Canada currently accepts two groups of self-employed applicants.

- Self-employed persons in athletics (see Tip # 31)
- Self-employed persons in cultural activities (see Tip # 32)

To fall under each category, a person needs to meet the following criteria (as per sections 88(1) and 100 to 105 of the Immigration and Refugee Protection Regulations):

- At least two years of acceptable self-employment or international activity in the qualifying period

- The ability and intent to establish their self-employment business in Canada
- The ability to contribute to the Canadian economy because of their future business activities in our country
- Collecting enough number of points from the selection grid

The qualifying period begins five years before applying to the immigration authorities and ends when an officer decides the case. For example, if you submit your application on June 1, 2019, and the officer makes a decision on your case on October 5, 2020, the qualifying period is from June 1, 2014, to October 5, 2020. It is impossible to predict the date an officer decides on the case. Consequently, you need to submit your documents only when you have accumulated at least two years of acceptable work experience.

The selection points do not play an important role in this method of immigration. You only need 35 points out of 100 points to qualify. Almost all refusals focus on the first three criteria only (i.e. experience, ability and intent, and contribution).

Here is a brief breakdown of the selections points:

- Education – up to 25 points
- Experience – up to 35 points
- Age – up to 10 points
- Ability in English or French languages – up to 24 points
- Adaptability (education or work in Canada, educated spouse or common-law partner, or having a qualifying family member in Canada) – up to 6 points

The self-employed stream is not an easy method of immigration. It targets professionals. If you do not qualify for any other stream of immigration to Canada, you may not replace them with this option. In other words, this method is not for someone who knows how to play the piano or how to play basketball. It is for professional pianists and basketball players or other professional or internationally acclaimed athletes and artists.

TIP # 31: IMMIGRATION TO CANADA FOR ATHLETES, COACHES, AND ATHLETIC EVENTS ORGANIZERS

Carlos is a professional soccer player from Guatemala. He has provided for himself and his family by playing soccer for the past six years. Carlos wants to move to Canada and start working as a self-employed soccer coach. He is looking for a possible option.

Athletes and professionals in athletic fields, such as coaches and referees, are one of the two major groups who could immigrate to Canada under the federal Self employed Program. People who are active in cultural activities may also immigrate to Canada under the Self-employed Program. The focus of this Tip is on athletics.

WHO IS A SELF-EMPLOYED ATHLETE?

Subsection 88(1) of the Immigration and Refugee Protection Regulations (IRPR) defines a self-employed person in athletics based on their relevant experience, their intention and ability to be self-employed in Canada, and significant contribution to the Canadian economy in respect to their self-employment activities.

RELEVANT EXPERIENCE

According to IRPR, relevant experience "means a minimum of two years of experience, during the period beginning five years before the date of application for a permanent resident visa and ending on the day an officer determination is made in respect of the application, consisting of.

(A) two one-year periods of experience in self-employment in athletics,

(B) two one-year periods of experience in participation at a world class level in athletics, or

(C) a combination of a one-year period of experience described in clause (A) and a one-year period of experience described in clause (B)"[12]

Imagine you submit your application to the immigration authorities on June 1, 2020. You need to roll back five years from that date (i.e. June 1, 2015). Then you need to prove that you had at least two years of relevant experience from June 1, 2015, to the date an immigration officer decides on your case.

For example, if you were a professional boxing champion in your country who covered your and your family (spouse and children) expenses through your athletic activities in 2017 and 2018, then you meet the test of relevant experience. Personal income via self-employed activities is a crucial factor in this area. Of course, if you are a world-renowned athlete and have competed at the world stage, then income becomes less important.

INTENTION AND ABILITY

The applicant needs to show they intend and can continue their self-employed activities in Canada. The immigration officers look into several factors to see if the applicant meets these requirements. For example, they consider the applicant's experience, their ties to Canadian athletic community, their correspondences with their Canadian counterparts, and if they have offered a business plan for what they intend to do in Canada. The officer also considers the net worth of the athlete and their financial stability.

SIGNIFICANT CONTRIBUTION

The concept of significant contribution is a broad and subjective matter. There is no financial threshold for significant contribution under this program. My experience shows the officers look into the experience of the applicant, their net worth, and their business plan to decide whether they will significantly contribute to the Canadian economy through their athletic activities or not.

WHAT ACTIVITIES ARE ATHLETICS?

NOC stands for National Occupational Classification. It is a classification system for jobs in Canada (see Tip # 16). Each classification has its 4-digit code. Athletic activities fall under one of the following NOC categories.

- NOC 5251: Athletes
- NOC 5252: Coaches
- NOC 5253: Sports officials and referees
- NOC 5254: Program leaders and instructors in recreation, sport and fitness

Use this list as a guideline only. Falling under one of these categories is not adequate for immigration under this group. You need to pass the tests of relevant experience, intention and ability, and significant contribution to meet the requirements of this category of immigration to Canada. There might be some exceptional situations where a person's job does not fall under any of these categories, yet the person may apply.

SELECTION POINTS

Applicants must meet the following three criteria to immigrate to Canada as self-employed persons in athletics. If the applicant does not meet any of the following, they won't receive the permanent residency of Canada.

- They need to meet all the requirements of a self-employed applicant (i.e. the relevant experience, the intention and ability, and the significant contribution elements).
- They need to acquire at least 35 points out of 100 points (see next page).
- They are not inadmissible to Canada due to security, criminality, financial matters, or medical issues (both the applicant and their dependent family members). See Tip # 81 for information on inadmissibility to Canada.

The following points apply to this group of applicants:

- Education: up to 25 points
- Work experience: up to 35 points

- Age: up to 10 points
- English or French proficiency: up to 24 points
- Adaptability: up to 6 points

If an individual has five years of self-employment experience, they will receive the minimum required 35 points. Consequently, they do not require points from other categories. As for English and French proficiency, any claim by an individual regarding their level of proficiency must include acceptable test results such as IELTS General or CELPIP for the English language and TEF Canada or TCF Canada for the French language.

AFTER ENTERING CANADA

Successful applicants under this program do not face any specific limitations regarding the kind of job they take, upon landing in Canada as permanent residents. However, if you genuinely do not intend to pursue self-employment, it means that you have committed misrepresentation (see Tip # 80).

THE COMPLEXITIES OF THIS METHOD

I have represented hundreds of clients under the self-employed program in the past eight years. In my opinion, this is one of the most challenging methods of immigration if an expert is not on your side. There are many complexities in proving your experience, intent, abilities, and contribution.

---

[12] Source: Immigration and Refugee Protection Regulations, SOR/2002-227, <http://canlii.ca/t/531vc> retrieved on 2017-12-25
Currency: This regulation is current to 2017-12-05 according to the Justice Laws Web Site

TIP # 32: IMMIGRATION TO CANADA FOR ARTISTS, PERFORMERS, AND SELF-EMPLOYED PEOPLE IN CULTURAL ACTIVITIES

Sofia is a German violin player. As a professional musician, she plays in various events. The event organizers compensate Sofia for her travel expenses and accommodation. They also pay her a lump sum of money for every performance. Sofia wants to immigrate to Canada. Two Canadian event organizers have agreed to arrange her tours of the country every year.

Canada is a multicultural society. Canadian government encourages the existence of different cultures next to each other. The cultural fabric of Canada is famously known as the cultural mosaic. Major cities of Canada such as Toronto, Montreal, Vancouver, Ottawa, and Winnipeg host people from thousands of cultural backgrounds. The Canadian immigration system also welcomes different cultures to the country. Subsection 3(b) of the Immigration and Refugee Protection Act (IRPA) defines one of the objectives of the Act "to enrich and strengthen the social and cultural fabric of Canadian society while respecting the federal, bilingual and multicultural character of Canada." Consequently, there are many options for artists to work and immigrate to Canada (see Tip # 52 for a comprehensive list). This Tip focuses on the main immigration option for artists.

DEFINE CULTURAL ACTIVITIES

It is difficult to define cultural activities, but the following list offers a loose sample of occupations that could fall under the umbrella of cultural activities. The numbers next to the classifications refer to the Canadian National Occupational Classification (NOC) codes (see Tip # 16).

NOC Code	Job Classification
5111	Librarians
5112	Conservators and curators
5113	Archivists
5211	Library and public archive technicians
5212	Technical occupations related to museums and art galleries
5121	Authors and writers
5122	Editors
5123	Journalists
5125	Translators, terminologists and interpreters
5131	Producers, directors, choreographers and related occupations
5132	Conductors, composers and arrangers
5133	Musicians and singers
5134	Dancers
5135	Actors and comedians
5136	Painters, sculptors and other visual artists
5221	Photographers
5222	Film and video camera operators
5223	Graphic arts technicians
5224	Broadcast technicians

NOC Code	Job Classification
5225	Audio and video recording technicians
5226	Other technical and co-ordinating occupations in motion pictures, broadcasting and the performing arts
5227	Support occupations in motion pictures, broadcasting, photography and the performing arts
5231	Announcers and other broadcasters
5232	Other performers, n.e.c.
5241	Graphic designers and illustrators
5242	Interior designers and interior decorators
5243	Theatre, fashion, exhibit and other creative designers
5244	Artisans and craftspersons
5245	Patternmakers textile, leather and fur products

This list is neither inclusive nor exclusive. A person may fall under any of the categories mentioned in the list, but not be a person who is involved in cultural activities. Some other activities that do not appear on the list such as architects and landscape architects might qualify, depending on their area of services.

WHO QUALIFIES?

A person qualifies as a self-employed applicant if they meet one of the following criteria in the past five years since their initial application reaches the IRCC office till the time the immigration officer decides on the application (subsection 88(1) of the Canadian Immigration Regulations).

(A) Two one-year periods of experience in self-employment in cultural activities, or

(B) two one-year periods of experience in participation at a world-class level in cultural activities, or

(C) a combination of one year of experience described in clause (A) and one year of experience described in clause (B).

Self-employed means the applicant was able to cover their expenses (themselves, their spouse, and their children) with their self-employment activities. It also means the person was not an employee of a specific employer. World-class is someone who is active at the highest global level (i.e. beyond their country and continent).

The applicant needs to show they will contribute to the Canadian economy via their cultural activities when they land in Canada. They must also show they intend to continue their self-employment in Canada. Also, see Tip # 31 about the following concepts:

- Intend and ability
- Significant contribution

THE PROCESS

The current process consists of two major steps.

1. The applicant submits their package to the Central Intake Office (CIO) in Canada. If CIO accepts the application, they will forward it to an overseas Visa Office.
2. The overseas Visa Office processes the application. If they approve the application, the applicant and their family members (spouse and dependent children) may enter Canada as permanent residents.

The self-employed category is a Federal immigration method. It means the applicant intends to live anywhere in Canada, but the province of Quebec. The processing time can vary depending on the merits of the application, the IRCC policies, the Visa Office policies, the completeness of the package, the complexities that may come along, etc. I have represented hundreds of applicants under this group and the processing time has been anywhere between 8 months to almost five years. Majority of my clients have faced processing times of less than two years though. Do not expect a quick response under this category.

THE COMPLEXITIES OF THIS METHOD

In my opinion, this is one of the most challenging methods of immigration if an expert is not on your side. A professional seasoned immigration consultant can assess your case objectively and present your case to the immigration authorities in a professional lawful manner. Don't take this matter lightly.

TIP # 33: THE START-UP VISA IMMIGRATION

Javier is a computer programmer from Spain. Javier recently came up with the idea of an innovative app for iPhone and Android cell phones. His app may also run on tablet and desktop environments. Javier believes his app will revolutionize the way we purchase our grocery in the future. He has deeply researched the global market and believes he can sell this product to giant companies such as Walmart, 7-Eleven, and Carrefour. Javier wants to establish his business in Canada to have easy access to the North American and South American markets. He also knows that treaties such as CETA could help him easily access the European market as a Canadian business. Javier has heard about an immigration option to Canada called Start-Up Visa. He knows this program could help him immigrate to Canada and even a get a work permit upfront to start his business as quick as possible.

Start-Up Visa immigration program targets entrepreneurs and innovative business people. The purpose is to encourage these people to immigrate to Canada and create businesses that could succeed locally and globally. IRCC is looking for the next big success story, similar to Google or Apple, get established in Canada via this program. Of course, not every start-up will turn into Google, but at least the idea needs to be big and plausible.

LETTER OF SUPPORT FROM A DESIGNATED ORGANIZATION

IRCC selects a group of organizations to evaluate and potentially support Start-Up Visa ideas. These organizations fall under three different groups:

- Venture capital funds
- Angel investor groups
- Business incubators

The most difficult phase of the Start-Up Visa program is to convince a *designated organization* to offer you a *letter of support*. You need to work on your business plan and try to perfect it. Then approach any of the designated organizations and try to receive their support. Then you may continue applying for your permanent residency and interim work permit. See Tip # 34 for more information on designated organizations.

Keep in mind, if an organization approves your idea and supports you, then you may not add new partners to the business, so make up your mind before approaching a designated organization.

ACCEPTABLE BUSINESS

An acceptable business needs to meet the following.

- The business idea must receive a letter of support from a designated organization
- Each immigration applicant needs to own at least 10% of the voting shares of the business
- The minimum combined voting shares for the applicants and the designated organization needs to be at least 51% of the total voting shares
- The applicant's role must be integral to the management and day to day operations of the business
- You need to incorporate the business in Canada

The maximum number of applicants per application is five. Each of them needs to meet all the requirements, so be careful with adding people to the application.

MINIMUM LANGUAGE REQUIREMENTS FOR THE START-UP VISA IMMIGRATION

You need to take at least one of the following tests.

- CELPIP: Canadian English Language Proficiency Index Program (Only CELPIP General is acceptable. Don't take General-LS)
- IELTS: International English Language Testing System (Only IELTS General is acceptable. Don't take IELTS Academic)
- TEF Canada: Test d'évaluation de français
- TCF Canada: Test de connaissance du français

You only need to take one of the tests per language. If you present multiple test results under the same language, the officer considers the latest test results. They won't combine the results.

The following table shows the minimum scores under each ability of the language tests for the Start-Up Visa program applicants.

Test	Language	Speaking	Listening	Reading	Writing
CELPIP	English	5	5	5	5
IELTS General	English	5.0	5.0	4.0	5.0
TEF Canada	French	225	180	150	225
TCF Canada	French	6	369	375	6

The figures above are minimums. You need to meet the minimum under each ability (i.e. speaking, listening, reading, and writing). Even if your score falls under the minimum for one of the abilities, you may not apply. Of course, the higher your score, the better, because of the following reasons.

- The immigration officer will have a better feeling about your application
- You can run your business more effectively in Canada, as you know our official languages better

SETTLEMENT FUNDS

There are no minimum investment funds for the Start-Up Visa. However, consider the following:

- Legal mandates
- IRCC expectations
- Designated organizations expectations

LEGAL MANDATES

Under subsection 12(2) of the Immigration and Refugee Protection Act (IRPA), "a foreign national may be selected as a member of the economic class by their ability to become economically established in Canada." As a result of this section of the law, your application must convince the officer you do not intend to use social welfare when you move to Canada.

You also need to meet the requirements of section 39 of IRPA, where it says, "A foreign national is inadmissible for financial reasons if they are or will be unable or unwilling to support themself or any other person who is dependent on them, and have not satisfied an officer that adequate arrangements for care and support, other than those that involve social assistance, have been made".

Considering these important sections of IRPA, you need to both shows you have the financial means and the ability to be financially self-sustained in Canada.

IRCC EXPECTATIONS

IRCC expects you to have minimum settlement funds per LICO table (see Tip # 29).

Keep in mind these are the minimums.

DESIGNATED ORGANIZATIONS EXPECTATIONS

Although there is no minimum investment for this method of immigration, the designated organization may demand certain capital investment in the business from your side. Generally speaking, the majority of successful people under this program are wealthy business owners, and they spend hundreds if not millions of dollars in Canada.

APPLICATION PROCESS FOR START-UP VISA

You need to follow these steps to become a permanent resident of Canada under the Start-Up Visa program. The exact steps could vary depending on your circumstances.

1. Come up with the business idea.
2. Perfect your business plan and approach a designated organization. You may need to register your corporation in Canada and also transfer funds during this process. Most applicants need to visit Canada before receiving a letter of support.
3. Get the letter of support from the designated organization.
4. Initiate the immigration application process.
5. Apply for a work permit. If you receive the work permit, you may start your business even before becoming a permanent resident of Canada.

If you meet the requirements of this method of application and if you are not inadmissible to Canada, you could become a permanent resident. See Tip # 81 for more details on inadmissibility.

The federal immigration programs such as the Start-Up Visa are for people who want to settle in any province or territory of Canada, but Quebec.

TIP # 34: DESIGNATED ORGANIZATIONS FOR THE START-UP VISA IMMIGRATION

Aruzhan is a successful businesswoman from Kazakhstan. She has recently invented a document management system and piloted the system through her network of businesses in Kazakhstan. Aruzhan has many success stories with this system. She wants to make her invention global. As a result, she intends to pitch her idea to a Canadian organization and eventually immigrate to Canada. She wonders which organizations best fit this plan.

The Start-up Visa program targets entrepreneurs and innovative business people. It is a federal immigration program for those who intend to immigrate to Canada, and their destination is anywhere but the province of Quebec. A key component of the Start-up Visa program is to receive a *Letter of Support* from a designated organization by IRCC (Immigration, Refugees and Citizenship Canada). These organizations fall under three major groups:

- **Venture capital funds** – According to bdc.ca[13], "a venture capital (VC) fund is a sum of money investors commit for investment in early-stage companies. The investors who supply the fund with money are designated as limited partners. The person who manages the fund is called the general partner. The general partner decides which early-stage companies the fund will invest in based on criteria established by the fund partners". A valid letter of support from a designated venture capital fund means they agreed to invest in your idea a minimum amount of CAD 200,000.

- **Angel investor groups** – A group of angel investors create an angel investor group. According to bdc.ca[14], angel investors "are wealthy, experienced businesspeople who invest their time and money in your high-growth business in exchange for equity." IRCC expects a minimum of CAD 75,000 along with a letter of support from a designated angel investor group to consider the letter acceptable.

- **Business incubators** – According to bdc.ca[15], "a business incubator is a program that gives very early stage companies access to mentorship, investors and other support to help them get established." Business incubators usually do not invest capital in business but offer their services to them. Acceptance by a business incubator and a letter of support from them without any investment is good enough for IRCC.

You only need one letter of support from one designated organization. For example, if you receive the letter from an incubator, you do not need a letter from a venture capitalist or an angel investor.

The following lists show the existing designated organizations for the Start-Up Visa program. I copied them verbatim from the IRCC website on February 18, 2019. Please visit their website for the official version. The following list is not official and not endorsed by IRCC. The following link redirects you the appropriate page.

settler.ca/88/sudo

VENTURE CAPITAL FUNDS

- BDC Venture Capital
- Celtic House Venture Partners
- Extreme Venture Partners LLP
- Golden Venture Partners Fund, LP
- Impression Ventures
- Information Venture Partners Management Inc.

- Innovation Platform Capital International LP
- iNovia Capital Inc.
- Lumira Capital
- Nova Scotia Innovation Corporation (o/a Innovacorp)
- OMERS Ventures Management Inc.
- Pangaea Ventures Ltd.
- PRIVEQ Capital Funds
- Real Ventures
- Relay Ventures
- ScaleUp Venture Partners, Inc.
- Top Renergy Inc.
- Vanedge Capital Limited Partnership
- Version One Ventures
- Westcap Management Ltd.
- Yaletown Venture Partners Inc.

ANGEL INVESTOR GROUPS

- Canadian International Angel Investors
- Ekagrata Inc.
- Golden Triangle Angel Network
- Keiretsu Forum Canada
- Oak Mason Investments Inc.
- Southeastern Ontario Angel Network
- TenX Angel Investors Inc.
- VANTEC Angel Network Inc.
- York Angel Investors Inc.

BUSINESS INCUBATORS

- Alacrity Foundation
- Alberta Agriculture and Forestry:
    - Agrivalue Processing Business Incubator
    - Food Processing Development Centre
- Biomedical Commercialization Canada Inc. (operating as Manitoba Technology Accelerator)
- Calgary Technologies Inc.
- Creative Destruction Lab
- Empowered Startups Ltd.
- Extreme Innovations
- Genesis Centre
- Highline BETA Inc.
- Innovacorp
- Interactive Niagara Media Cluster o/a Innovate Niagara
- Invest Ottawa
- Knowledge Park o/a Planet Hatch
- LatAm Startups
- Launch Academy - Vancouver
- LaunchPad PEI Inc.
- Millworks Centre for Entrepreneurship
- NEXT Canada
- North Forge Technology Exchange
- Real Investment Fund III L.P. o/a FounderFuel
- Ryerson Futures Inc.
- Spark Commercialization and Innovation Centre
- Spring Activator

- The DMZ at Ryerson University
- Toronto Business Development Centre (TBDC)
- TSRV Canada Inc. (operating as Techstars Canada)
- VIATEC
- Waterloo Accelerator Centre
- York Entrepreneurship Development Institute

Read Tip # 33 for more details on Start-Up Visa immigration to Canada.

---

[13] Source: https://www.bdc.ca/en/articles-tools/entrepreneur-toolkit/templates-business-guides/glossary/pages/venture-capital-fund.aspx
[14] Source: https://www.bdc.ca/en/articles-tools/start-buy-business/start-business/pages/angel-investors-how-find-them.aspx
[15] Source: https://www.bdc.ca/en/articles-tools/entrepreneur-toolkit/templates-business-guides/glossary/pages/business-incubators.aspx

TIP # 35: TWO-STAGE IMMIGRATION FOR OTHER SELF-EMPLOYED AND ENTREPRENEURS

Erick is a businessman from Bolivia. He has a total net asset of $1,000,000. He wants to establish a business in Canada that promotes Bolivian culture. Erick believes his company will generate jobs for several Canadians. He prefers to start working in Canada as quickly as possible. However, he hopes that this process helps him become a permanent resident of Canada eventually.

If you have a business mind and enough expertise you could immigrate to Canada in two stages.

Stage 1.   Receiving a temporary work permit under the IMP Code C11

Stage 2.   Immigrating to Canada under the Express Entry System

Please read this Tip carefully and remember, the immigration policies could change at any time. An option that is available today may vanish tomorrow.

STAGE 1 – WORK PERMIT UNDER THE IMP CODE C11

The *International Mobility Program (IMP)* paves the way to apply for a Work Permit without a Labour Market Impact Assessment (LMIA). The LMIA process is tedious and prone to refusal. Consequently, about two-thirds of those who receive Canadian work permits use one of the IMP programs (e.g. the Mobility Francophone, etc.). One of the IMP options is the LMIA exemption code C11. This code is for entrepreneurs or self-employed people who meet the following requirements:

- They have the skills and background to establish a successful business in Canada or purchase an existing one and expand it
- They own at least 50% of the business they establish or purchase in Canada
- Their activities in Canada create significant cultural, social, or economic benefits to our country (e.g. contributes to remote areas, creates jobs for Canadians, exports Canadian goods to other countries, contributes to technological development, is innovative, helps Canadians to hone their skills, etc.)
- They present a business plan that is meaningful and viable
- They have taken steps to make their plans happen before entering Canada (e.g. they have established the business, they have secured enough financial resources for the business, they have contacted parallel businesses in Canada, they have signed agreements with Canadian suppliers, etc.)[16]

This work permit may cover one or at most two applicants as the applicant needs to hold at least 50% voting shares of the business.

STAGE 2 – APPLYING FOR PERMANENT RESIDENCY

IMP Code C11 work permit does not result in permanent residency by default. IRCC has limited the dual intention for permanent residency under this code to the following options:

- Immigration to Canadian provinces as a business person or entrepreneur (PNP programs)
- Immigration to Quebec as a self-employed person

Despite limitations on dual intent, an applicant who moves to Canada under this program and works for at least one year could apply under the category of Federal Skilled Worker program through the Express Entry system. To apply for permanent residency, you need to meet the following criteria:

- Actively manage your business in Canada for at least 12 consecutive months in Canada with a valid work permit. This option is important as you will receive up to 340 CRS points (conditions apply – subject to change in the future)

- Meet the minimum requirements for the Federal Skilled Worker Program (FSWP).

- Enter the Express Entry pool and receive an Invitation to Apply (ITA) from IRCC

I must emphasize that your intention, in the beginning, needs to be the Work Permit alone. If after a year of work experience you decide to immigrate to Canada, you may consider stage 2. I also encourage you to read Tip # 23 and 24 for the minimum requirements of the FSWP program.

WHAT HAPPENS TO THE FAMILY OF THE APPLICANT?

If you receive a work permit to Canada which is valid for at least six months your spouse qualifies to apply for an open work permit which allows her to work in Canada for any employer. Your minor children could also study in Canada without a study permit. Of course, an immigration officer has the final say to issue a work permit or visa for your dependent family members.

---

[16] Source: https://www.canada.ca/en/immigration-refugees citizenship/corporate/publications-manuals/operational-bulletins-manuals/temporary-residents/foreign-workers/exemption-codes/canadian-interests-significant-benefit-entrepreneurs-self-employed-candidates-seeking-operate-business-r205-c11.html

TIP # 36: IMMIGRATION UNDER THE PROVINCIAL NOMINEE PROGRAM (PNP)

Marie is an international student from Belgium. She is currently completing her master's degree at Dalhousie University in Halifax, Nova Scotia. A local employer has offered Marie a full-time job upon completion of her studies. Marie wants to take the job and also immigrate to Canada. She wonders if the province of Nova Scotia could help her fulfill her dreams.

Canada has ten provinces and three territories. The provinces of Canada are Alberta, British Columbia, Manitoba, New Brunswick, Newfoundland and Labrador, Nova Scotia, Ontario, Prince Edward Island, Quebec, and Saskatchewan. The territories are Northwest Territories, Nunavut, and Yukon. The territories are more dependent on the federal government of Canada than the provinces.

THE BASICS

Most provinces and territories have special immigration programs to attract population, skills, and money to their provinces. Provincial Nominee Program or PNP is the common phrase referring to these programs.

Quebec has the strongest immigration programs in place. They do not refer to their programs as PNP. The Quebec government deal with all aspects of immigration to their province. Although the final decision-maker is a federal immigration officer, they generally do not interfere with the selection process conducted by the Quebec officers.

The federal government of Canada negotiates with the provinces and puts limitations on PNPs. For example, they put a cap on the number of applicants each province may select. They also screen applicants for inadmissibility to Canada and their ability to establish themselves economically in Canada. If the federal officer decides to refuse an application, they get in touch with the provincial officer first and consult with them.

One of the reasons for PNPs is to distribute population in all different regions of Canada. As a result, if an area traditionally receives few immigrants, the federal government may loosen up their criteria for getting provincial nominees. Consequently, an applicant who does not qualify for immigration under federal programs may be eligible to immigrate to Canada under a provincial program.

THE INTENT

When someone applies for a PNP, they must show they intend to live in the province they have selected. For example, if you apply for Manitoba PNP, you must demonstrate to the officer you plan to move to Manitoba. Provinces may ask you to take some steps to ensure the integrity of the PNP system. Some examples include signing intent or performance agreements; visiting the province before immigration; or showing strong ties with the province such as close family members or valid job offers.

THE PROCEDURE

A typical PNP application goes like this.

1. The applicant shows interest to the province (normally by submitting an online form).
2. The province invites potential applicants to apply.
3. The applicant submits several forms and documents to the province.
4. The province issues Certificate of Nomination for the selected candidates.
5. The applicant submits several forms and documents to IRCC.

6. IRCC reviews the application and allows successful applicants to enter Canada as permanent residents.

The preceding steps do not apply to every PNP. Sometimes the first step is not necessary. Sometimes the candidate enters Canada on a work permit which eventually could turn into permanent residency.

PNP EXPRESS ENTRY

Some provinces accept a few applicants via the Express Entry system. You usually need to enter the pool of Express Entry first. Then either the province picks you automatically, or you have to approach the province and show your interest. If a province selects you, you will receive 600 CRS points which guarantees an Invitation to Apply (ITA). See Tip # 22 for more information about Express Entry.

THE TARGET

If you want to apply under PNP, you need to keep an eye on opportunities that arise in the province of your choice. The following links redirect you to the PNP websites.

- Alberta: settler.ca/88/pnp/ab
- British Columbia: settler.ca/88/pnp/bc
- Manitoba: settler.ca/88/pnp/mb
- New Brunswick: settler.ca/88/pnp/nb
- Newfoundland and Labrador: settler.ca/88/pnp/nl
- Nova Scotia: settler.ca/88/pnp/ns
- Ontario: settler.ca/88/pnp/on
- Prince Edward Island: settler.ca/88/pnp/pe
- Quebec: settler.ca/88/pnp/qc
- Saskatchewan: settler.ca/88/pnp/sk
- Northwest Territories: settler.ca/88/pnp/nt
- Yukon: settler.ca/88/pnp/yt

The opportunities constantly change.

TIP # 37: FAMILY REUNIFICATION

Jacob is a US citizen. He started dating Michael, a Canadian citizen, four years ago. They initially met over a dating website, but then visited each other several times in Canada and the US. Jacob and Michael even travelled to Mexico once. They got married in Windsor, Ontario four months ago. Jacob wants to quit his job and move to Canada to live with his husband. They wonder if this is even possible.

One of the objectives of the Immigration and Refugee Protection Act is "to see that families are reunited in Canada" [paragraph 3(1)(d)]. That's probably why about 25 to 30 percent of all the newcomers to Canada immigrate under Family Reunification programs.

THE TWO SIDES OF FAMILY REUNIFICATION

A typical Family Reunification application consists of two sides,

- the sponsor
- the applicant and their dependent family members

An alternative term for family reunification is family sponsorship.

WHO IS THE SPONSOR?

A sponsor is someone who meets all the following requirements:

- Is a Canadian citizen or permanent resident
- is at least 18 years old
- is a resident of Canada (some exceptions apply)
- meets the income requirements (some exceptions apply),
- meets the good character requirements
- files a sponsorship application
- signs the undertaking agreement: They agree to support their family members for several years after landing in Canada as permanent residents.

Foreign nationals such as international students or foreign workers are not eligible to sponsor their family members to Canada.

Of course, the devil is in the details. There are many limitations and exceptions to the conditions above.

WHO IS THE APPLICANT?

As you probably can guess, the applicant is the person who wants to immigrate to Canada. This person could be any of the following about the sponsor.

- A Spouse, common-law partner, or conjugal partner who is at least 18 years old at the time of filing the sponsorship application
- A father or mother
- A grandfather or grandmother
- A dependent child (i.e. under 22 years old and not married – some exceptions apply)
- A brother, sister, nephew, niece, or grandchild who is under 18 years old and orphaned
- An adopted child who is under 18 years old

- Some other family members under special circumstances

Keep in mind, the definition of a family member under the immigration law could be different from the definition of a family member under the other laws. You also need to remember; some circumstances could affect the eligibility of family members.

WHO IS A DEPENDENT FAMILY MEMBER?

When you sponsor your family members, they may have dependent family members of their own. For example, you are sponsoring your mother, but she is married to your stepfather. In this situation, you may sponsor them both, or rather your mom and her dependent family members who happen to be her spouse. Eligible dependent family members of an applicant could be any of the following.

- Their spouse or common-law partner
- Their dependent children
- Their spouse or common-law partner's dependent children
- Their adopted dependent children

Dependent family members may or may not accompany the applicant. In other words, they may choose not to immigrate to Canada. A dependent child is usually a child who is under 22 years old and not married (exceptions apply).

TIP # 38: SPOUSE, CONJUGAL AND COMMON-LAW PARTNER

Sergej is a citizen of Turkmenistan. He has been dating Galina, a Canadian citizen, for the past two years over the internet. Sergej and Galina have fallen in love. They want to live together in Canada. Sergej wonders if Galina could sponsor him to Canada.

The Canadian immigration laws and regulations consider three groups of people to be in marriage-like relationships.

- Spouses
- Conjugal partners
- Common-law partners

The relationship is valid between two persons who are of opposite or same sexes. If your relationship does not fall under any of the above categories you may not immigrate to Canada under spousal sponsorship, but what are those relationships exactly?

SPOUSES

Spouses are two persons that are legally married. Both parties must be present at the same location when the marriage takes place (some exceptions apply). The local authorities must consider the marriage valid (e.g. if the local authorities do not authorize same-sex marriage, then the marriage is not valid). Spouses hold a document usually called a "marriage certificate" which explains the details of the marriage such as the date it has come into effect, the location, and its validity.

CONJUGAL PARTNERS

Conjugal partners are two persons who are committed to each other and in conjugal relationship to each other for at least one full year. Conjugal partners show the characteristics of two married persons, such as:

- an intimate and sexual relationship
- commitment
- attending parties together
- travelling together
- spending their time together as much as possible
- supporting each other financially and emotionally

This list is not exhaustive. Also, none of the items on the list is conclusive. You need to look at the quality of the relationship the two persons present to realize whether you can consider them conjugal partners or not. The conclusion is to some extent subjective. Therefore, if you would like to apply under this category, make sure to present as much evidence as possible.

Conjugal partners usually do not live under the same roof or even in the same country due to valid reasons. For example, if one of them has immigrated to Canada and the other one lives abroad and is not able to travel to Canada because of reasons other than inadmissibility. Some countries prohibit same-sex couples from living together. Such laws prohibit or at least limit cohabitation.

COMMON-LAW PARTNERS

Common-law partners are conjugal partners who have lived together for at least one full year. If you are in a common-law relationship with another person, you need to show that you have shared the same place for living. You also need to show other evidence that helps the visa officer to confirm your conjugal relationship. Joint rent agreements or a house in both names would be very helpful.

HOW TO VERIFY A MARITAL RELATIONSHIP

If you are legally married a marriage certificate could suffice to verify your relationship. However, when it comes to sponsoring your spouse or if you are in a common-law or conjugal relationship, then you need to consider as much evidence as possible. The following list shows some indications of conjugal, common-law, or spousal relationships:

- A common biological or adopted child
- Apartment rental agreement under both names
- A property deed under both names
- Joint bank accounts
- Travel tickets or bookings to the same destination for both
- Pictures of your wedding reception or ceremony (if applicable)
- Pictures of the places you have visited or the parties you have attended
- Life insurance policies that one of you is the beneficiary of the other
- Letters of attestation by your friends or family members
- Any other document that could prove your financial or emotional dependency on each other

This list is neither inclusive nor exclusive. You need to have all necessary information handy to show the officer that you are really in conjugal relations with each other. The officer also considers some other factors such as,

- How you initially met
- For how long you knew each other before considering the conjugal relationship
- Your local traditions and if you have followed them or not
- Are you from the same background or ethnicity?
- ...

Again, none of the above could verify if your relationship is valid for immigration. People have the freedom to choose their ways of living no matter how odd their decisions appear to the officer or how deviated they are from social norms. A reasonable officer and a group of convincing documents could ease your way to verify your true relationship. See Tips 39 and 40 for more information about spousal sponsorship.

TIP # 39: CAN I SPONSOR MY SPOUSE (WIFE/HUSBAND) TO IMMIGRATE TO CANADA?

Sabrina, an Iraqi citizen, is in love with her husband, Ahmed. Since Ahmed is a permanent resident of Canada, he wishes to take Sabrina with her to Canada.

One of the objectives of the IRPA or rather the Immigration and Refugee Protection Act of Canada is "to see that families are reunited in Canada" (see s.3(1)(d) of the IRPA). The Act further describes Family Reunification as an acceptable method of immigration under subsection 12(1):

IRPA s.12(1) Family Reunification "A foreign national may be selected as a member of the family class by their relationship as the spouse, common-law partner, child, parent or other prescribed family member of a Canadian citizen or permanent resident."

As you can see a spouse (a husband or wife) or a common-law partner is considered to be a family member under the immigration law. Therefore, if you are a Canadian Citizen or Permanent Resident who qualifies to sponsor a family member, then you may sponsor your spouse to immigrate to Canada and become a permanent resident.

WHO IS A SPOUSE OR COMMON-LAW PARTNER?

A spouse or common-law partner is a foreign national who meets certain requirements. See Tip # 38 for more details. Also, see Tip # 7 for the definition of foreign nationals.

WHO CAN SPONSOR THEIR SPOUSE?

To qualify as a sponsor, you need to meet certain criteria. The "Immigration and Refugee Protection Regulations" (Part 7 Division 3) outlines such criteria. For example, you must,

- be a Canadian citizen or permanent resident
- be at least 18 years old
- reside in Canada (under certain conditions you may not reside in Canada at the time of application)
- file the sponsorship application according to the guidelines
- do not owe the government of Canada or your provincial government money or other obligations due to previous sponsorships
- not be in another marital relationship at the time of marrying to your spouse or applying for your spouse

There are many other applicable conditions. For example, you need to show that your application is genuine, and you intend to reunite with your spouse. If the sponsor is in jail or has committed certain offences, they will be disqualified. See Tip # 40 for more details on conditions that apply to sponsors.

TIP # 40: WHO IS A SPOUSAL SPONSOR FOR IMMIGRATION TO CANADA?

Mark, a Canadian citizen, has recently married to Cuban citizen. He wants to sponsor her newlywed spouse to Canada. However, Mark has a criminal history. He assaulted his ex-wife brutally and served three-month jail time. He wonders if his history affects his sponsorship application.

Some Canadians or Permanent Residents of Canada sponsor their partners (legally marries spouses, common-law partners, or conjugal partners) for immigration to Canada. You learned those relationships under Tip # 38. Here I focus on the characteristics of a potential sponsor. As a general rule, a sponsor is,

- a citizen or permanent resident (PR) of Canada
- if a PR resides in Canada and if a citizen either resides in Canada or intends to move back to Canada when his or her spouse becomes a permanent resident
- is at least 18 years old
- has not been sponsored to Canada as a spouse in the past five

years

- promises to support his or her spouse for three years from the day they land in Canada
- promises to support his or her spouse's children for ten years or till they are 25 (if they are 22 years or older at the time of landing, for three years)
- is not subject to a removal order from Canada (see Tip # 73)
- is not in any prison, jail, penitentiary, or reformatory
- has not a conviction under any of the following offences inside or outside Canada:
    - a sexual offence or attempt to sexual offences against any person
    - physically harming family members, former spouses, their children, and certain other people
- is not an undischarged bankrupt
- is not in default of certain financial obligations to the government of Canada
- is not in receipt of social assistance for a reason other than disability
- files a sponsorship application and provides all necessary documents and signed forms.

I tried to keep the list as concise as possible. Make sure to consult with a professional, to make sure you meet the requirements.

TIP # 41: IMMIGRATION OF PARENTS TO CANADA VIA SPONSORSHIP

Cirus is a permanent resident of Canada. He landed in Canada three years ago. Cirus is single. He just recently finished his college diploma in Canada. Cirus feels very lonely. He wants to sponsor his mother to Canada so she can stay with him. Cirus's father passed away two years ago, and his mother has no close relatives in their home country. Cirus doesn't know if he qualifies to initiate the sponsorship process.

Majority of people who immigrate to Canada are economic immigrants (e.g. under the Express Entry program). About 25 to 30% of the immigrants fall under the family reunification programs. About 20% of the sponsored immigrants are parents or grandparents of Canadians or permanent residents of Canada. The rest are mostly spouses or common-law partners or other family members. The Government of Canada intends to accept more than 20,000 parents or grandparents to Canada every year (subject to change). These parents and grandparents become permanent residents of Canada upon landing to our country, but how this process works.

WHO COULD BE A SPONSOR?

According to sections 130 to 134 of the Immigration and Refugee Protection Regulations (IRPR), a sponsor in this context refers to a Canadian Citizen or Permanent Citizen of Canada who meets the following requirements:

- Is at least 18 years old

- Lives in Canada not outside Canada

- Accepts to sign an undertaking pledge for 20 years (i.e. in the next 20 years from the day of applicant's landing the sponsor will financially provide for their parents or grandparents. The applicants may not use social assistance to cover their expenses for the first 20 years of their presence in Canada)

- Is not subject to a removal order from Canada (see Tip # 73)

- Is not in any reformatory, prison, jail, or penitentiary

- Has no criminal record of the violent or sexual nature toward people close to the sponsor (details are beyond the scope of this book)

- Is not an undischarged bankrupt

- Is not in receipt of social assistance for a reason other than disability

- Does not owe money to the Canadian governments (details are beyond the scope of this book)

- Has filed their taxes in Canada and their income on Notice of Assessment in the last three consecutive years is at least 30% above the poverty line based on the number of people they are sponsoring, their household, and their dependents. See Tip # 42 for more details.

If the sponsor does not meet the financial requirements, they could ask their spouse or common-law partner to be a co-signer of the application. The immigration officers consider the sum of income for the sponsor and the co-signer for each year. In return, the co-signer accepts a similar duration of the undertaking.

WHO COULD BE AN APPLICANT?

For parental sponsorship, an applicant is a person who is a foreign national and is the parent or grandparent of the sponsor. There are no specific age limitations, but the applicant needs to be admissible to Canada. The grounds of inadmissibility as laid out under sections 33 to 43 of the Immigration and Refugee Protection Act (IRPA) are the following:

- Security (e.g. someone who is a terrorist)
- Human or international rights violations (e.g. someone who kills a large group of people because of their gender or religious beliefs)
- Serious criminality (e.g. someone who commits an offence in Canada and serves a jail time of more than six months)
- Criminality (e.g. someone who commits an indictable offence)
- Organized criminality (e.g. someone who is a member of a criminal gang)
- Health grounds (e.g. someone who has a disease that could put the health or safety of Canadians at risk)
- Financial reasons (e.g. if the applicant intends to file for social assistance upon landing in Canada)
- Misrepresentation (e.g. if the applicant lies to the officer)
- Other matters (e.g. not appearing for an immigration examination)

See Tips 80 to 82 for information on inadmissibility.

WHAT IS THE PROCESS?

Since the Government changes the process constantly, visit the IRCC website or *settler.ca* for the up-to-date information on the process.

TIP # 42: MINIMUM NECESSARY INCOME FOR SPONSORING PARENTS

Sonia immigrated to Canada six years ago. She is a Canadian citizen now. Sonia is married and has a child. Both Sonia and her husband are professionals. Sonia is an IT manager at a well-known financial institution, and her husband is a Professional Engineer who works full-time for a construction company. Sonia wonders, if she could sponsor her parents to Canada. She wonders if there is a minimum necessary income to be an eligible sponsor.

Canadian citizens or permanent residents of Canada who sponsor their parents or grandparents to Canada need to meet certain financial requirements. Consider the following:

- The filing date of the application is extremely important. The filing date is the day your initial sponsorship application package reaches the immigration office (e.g. May 9, 2019).

- The sponsor (i.e. the Canadian citizen or the permanent resident of Canada) needs to meet the minimum necessary income for the last three consecutive years immediately before the filing date (e.g. 2018, 2017, 2016).

- The sponsor's spouse or common-law partner may also co-sign the application. In this case, you may add both incomes together. No other family members may be a co-signer. The income of the parents is not important.

- The only acceptable source of verifying the income is the Canada Revenue Agency (CRA) Notice of Assessment (NOA) or its equivalent the Option C Printout. Look at line 150 of the NOA to calculate your income.

- If you are applying in January 2019, it is unlikely you have the NOA for 2018, so you need to rely on your income in 2015, 2016, and 2017. The law does not mandate you to go as far as 2015, but an operational bulletin (#561) recommends the officers to calculate the income this way.

- The minimum necessary income depends on the family size of the sponsor and includes the sponsored persons. For example, if the sponsor is single and she is sponsoring her mother, then the number is two. If the sponsor has a spouse and two dependent children and they are sponsoring her parents, then the number is six (i.e. the sponsor, the spouse, two children, and two parents).

The following table shows the minimum necessary income based on the number of family members.

Size of Family Unit	2015	2016	2017	2018
2 persons	$38,618	$39,371	$39,813	$40,379
3 persons	$47,476	$48,404	$48,945	$49,641
4 persons	$57,642	$58,768	$59,426	$60,271
5 persons	$65,377	$66,654	$67,400	$68,358
6 persons	$73,733	$75,174	$76,015	$77,095
7 persons	$82,091	$83,695	$84,631	$85,835
If more than 7 persons, for each additional person, add	$8,358	$8,522	$8,616	$8,740

These figures change year over year. Visit the following page for the updated figures.

settler.ca/88/mni

TIP # 43: SPONSORING SIBLINGS (BROTHERS OR SISTERS) TO CANADA

Masha is a Canadian citizen who is originally from Russia. She has a 12-year-old brother who lives in Saint Petersburg. Masha's parents died in a tragic car accident a few weeks ago. She now wants to sponsor her younger brother to Canada as he has no guardians in his home country.

Many Canadian Permanent Residents or Citizens are willing to sponsor their siblings (brothers or sisters) to Canada. Unfortunately, this option is not available to every brother or sister. Under certain circumstances this is possible. First of all, the person who would like to sponsor their sibling(s) needs to meet the following conditions:

- be a Canadian citizen or permanent resident
- be at least 18 years old
- resides in Canada
- files the sponsorship application according to the guidelines
- does not owe the government of Canada or his/her provincial government money or other obligations due to previous

sponsorship applications

- meets the minimum income requirements
- meets other requirements mentioned on Tip # 40 and 41

The preceding conditions are necessary but not enough. The following conditions also need to be in place:

- The parents of the sponsor are deceased (dead)
- The siblings are under 18 years of age

If the siblings are 18 years old or more, they still can be sponsored if the sponsor is a lonely person (they do not have a spouse, a common-law partner, a conjugal partner, a mother or father, a child, or any close relatives in Canada or who are eligible for sponsorship to Canada).

These are tough conditions but applicable to some people. If you believe that these conditions apply to you, then I recommend discussing your situation with an immigration consultant or lawyer for official advice.

Sometimes your only option is to sponsor your siblings under the Humanitarian and Compassionate grounds (see Tip # 47 for more information).

TIP # 44: REFUGEES AND PEOPLE IN NEED OF PROTECTION

Anaishe is a political activist from Zimbabwe. She recently was arrested and briefly detained by the police due to her open opposition to the government on Facebook. Anaishe fears she could be convicted and held in prison for an extended period. One of Anaishe's friends suggests she claims refugee status in Canada. Anaishe already holds a valid Study Permit to Canada. She returns to Canada to complete her studies, but she is not quite sure if she qualifies for seeking asylum.

Canada is a relatively welcoming country for refugees. For example, Canada accepted more than 40,000 refugees in 2017 which is about 14% of all the new immigrants to Canada. Refugees come to Canada under two major groups.

- **Resettlement**: These people are displaced from their country. They usually file refugee with the Office of the *United Nations High Commissioner for Refugees* (UNHCR). Canada accepts some of these refugees under its obligations to the United Nations. Resettled refugees enter Canada as permanent residents. The processing of such applications happens outside Canada (see Tip

#45 for more information).

- **Local claims**: Some people claim refugee status at a Canadian port of entry or while they are inside Canada. The authority that ultimately makes decisions about these people is the Immigration and Refugee Board of Canada (some exceptions apply).

TWO TYPES OF REFUGEES

The Immigration and Refugee Protection Act (IRPA) recognizes the following two types of refugees.

- **Convention Refugees** – These are people who do not live in their country. They are afraid of going back to their home country because their government may persecute them due to their race, religion, social group, political views or nationality (practitioners see section 96 of IRPA).

- **People who need protection** – This group are those people who have a fear of going back to their home country because they may face torture, unusual treatment, or even loss of their lives. People who need protection cannot trust their government to protect them against such issues (practitioners see section 97 of IRPA).

Please note that Canada does not tolerate fraudulent activities. Our country is a welcoming country to refugees, but we do not want people who file false claims to undermine the integrity of our immigration system. Any misrepresentation in an application could result in refusal or even prosecution.

TIP # 45: RESETTLEMENT TO CANADA

Aderito is a journalist and human rights activist from Mozambique. The riot police attacked his home a few months ago and severely beat him for his political views. It took Aderito a few months to recover from his injuries. Meanwhile, he received several death threats. Aderito, eventually, decided to flee the country. He reached out to the UNHCR office in Pretoria, South Africa and filed for protection. The UNHCR offered him asylum. However, he may not stay in South Africa. Aderito has two cousins in Calgary, Canada. He hopes to resettle there and start a new life. Aderito hopes for a brighter future that offers him freedom of speech.

Sometimes people are displaced from their home countries due to their nationality, race, political opinions, religion, or membership to a particular group (e.g. sexual orientation or gender). One option for those people is to seek asylum through The United Nations Refugee Agency (UNHCR). In some exceptional cases, you may still resettle to Canada if you receive support from a private sponsorship group, instead of the UNHCR. If their requests go through, you could potentially resettle to Canada and start a new life in our country. A successful resettlement process could lead to the permanent residency of Canada upon arrival.

If you are not familiar with the concept of refugees, read Tip # 44 first.

THREE SPONSORSHIP OPTIONS FOR RESETTLEMENT

If you pass the first hurdle of approval by the UNHCR, you then need to move to Canada via one of the following potential options.

- Government-Assisted Refugees Program (GAR)
- Private Sponsorship of Refugees Program (PSR)
- Blended Visa Office-Referred Program (BOVR)

GOVERNMENT-ASSISTED REFUGEES PROGRAM (GAR)

Under the GAR, a local Canadian visa office reviews the applicant's case. The officer may then interview the applicant. If they believe the Canadian government wants to sponsor the applicant, the applicant will go through the medical examination and criminal and security background checks. They also need to give biometrics. Assuming everything goes well, the applicant will be resettled to Canada as a permanent resident of Canada.

PRIVATE SPONSORSHIP OF REFUGEES PROGRAM (PSR)

Under this program, a community group in Canada or a group of five or more Canadians or permanent residents of Canada agree to sponsor the refugee for their first twelve months of staying in Canada. Of course, a successful applicant also needs to go through the medical examination, security screening, and biometrics before resettlement to Canada.

BLENDED VISA OFFICE-REFERRED PROGRAM (BOVR)

The BOVR option is a blend of the GAR and PSR options, in which the government supports the applicant for six months, and the private sector supports them for another six months.

TIP # 46: CLAIMING REFUGEE STATUS

Noura is a citizen of Saudi Arabia. She is married but has no children of her own. Noura was only 12 years old when she was forced to marry her abusive husband. She is 21 years old now. Noura and her husband travelled to Canada as visitors two months ago.

Noura's husband was beating her with a belt when the neighbouring hotel room residents reported them to the local Canadian police. The police intervened and transferred Noura to the nearest women's shelter in Hamilton, Ontario. Consequently, Noura has the fear to go back to her husband. She believes neither the Saudi authorities nor her family will protect her against him.

Noura has a genuine fear of dying at the hands of her husband shortly. She wonders if she could stay in Canada in an open society that respects women's rights and freedoms. Noura wonders if she could claim refugee status in Canada.

Some refugees file for asylum at a port of entry or while they are in Canada. If their request goes through, they could eventually become permanent residents of Canada. They may even later become naturalized citizens. In this article, we review refugee claims both at a port of entry and inside Canada.

CLAIMING REFUGEE STATUS AT A PORT OF ENTRY

The Border Services Officers (BSO) examine every single person who intends to enter Canada at a port of entry. If you claim refugee status, the BSO takes the following steps:

1. Decides whether they need to use the services of an interpreter or not. Many BSOs speak non-official languages of Canada, especially if you are crossing a major port of entry such as Toronto Lester Pearson airport.

2. Asks you if you need representation. For example, you may hire a lawyer or an RCIC to help you (see Tip # 11 for the differences between lawyers and RCICs).

3. Reviews the IRCC, CBSA, and the police databases to see if anything related to your history or identity is available.

4. If necessary, consults with the visa office responsible for your country of origin.

5. Takes your biometrics (see Tip # 12 for more information on biometrics).

6. Searches and reviews your documents.

7. Decides on how to proceed.

Generally speaking, there will be three potential scenarios at this point:

- The BSO gives you 15 days or so to complete all necessary forms (such as the Basis of Claim) and documents. She or he also refers you to the Immigration and Refugee Board of Canada (IRB) for a refugee hearing and decision; or

- The BSO detains you for further investigation or interviews. Detention could occur because of inadmissibility reasons or lack of proper documentation; or

- The BSO directs you back to the United States. Removal to the US only happens if you are entering Canada via the US and you are not exempt from the Safe Third Country rules.

CLAIMING REFUGEE STATUS INSIDE CANADA

If you are already inside Canada, you may visit an inland IRCC office and file for asylum. In this situation, you need to have all the necessary forms and documents ready. The immigration officer reviews your forms and documents, runs an interview with you, and if finds you eligible, refers you to the IRB.

THE PROCESS OF REFUGEE CLAIMS

The process of refugee claims varies depending on your country of origin and how your first hearing goes. However, a smooth version of the process is the following.

1. You attend a refugee hearing at the Refugee Protection Division of the IRB.
2. If they approve your claim, you become a protected person.
3. You will apply for Canadian permanent residency (PR). You may even add your dependent family members to the PR application.

The immigration authorities may refuse or approve the refugee claims of certain people without hearing because of their country of origin. IRCC sets the policies of designated countries and reviews those policies every now and again.

In real life, matters could get a lot more complicated. The CBSA may even deport you from Canada.

TIP # 47: HUMANITARIAN AND COMPASSIONATE GROUNDS

Amani is a citizen of the Republic of South Sudan. He was an international student in Canada when South Sudan gained its independence in 2011. Amani was a successful student and completed his master's degree in Canada. He started working in Canada on a Post-Graduate Work Permit. Unfortunately, doctors diagnosed Amani with a rare disease six months ago. Since the disease is a huge financial burden for the Canadian immigration system, Amani will be inadmissible to Canada on health grounds. South Sudan won't be able to offer Amani the treatments he needs. On the other hand, he has established himself in Canada in the past few years. Amani wonders if he could immigrate to Canada under Humanitarian and Compassionate Grounds (H&C), hoping the government ignores his medical inadmissibility.

The Canadian immigration system offers many opportunities for immigration. Despite all those opportunities, this system is full of limitations. One of the limitations is inadmissibility to Canada. If a person is inadmissible to Canada, they may not immigrate to Canada, even if they meet all the requirements. There are nine main reasons for inadmissibility, namely:

1. Security;

2. Human or international rights violations;
3. Serious criminality;
4. Criminality;
5. Organized criminality;
6. Health grounds;
7. Financial reasons;
8. Misrepresentation; and
9. Non-compliance with the Immigration Act (see Tip #81 for more information on inadmissibility).

Sometimes the applicant is not admissible, but they do not fully meet the requirements of an immigration option to Canada. In both situations, (i.e. inadmissibility or not meeting the requirements), a person could immigrate to Canada under the Humanitarian and Compassionate Grounds (H&C).

WHAT IS H&C?

Suppose you want to immigrate to Canada, but you do not meet the requirements of an application, or you are inadmissible to Canada. In this situation, if you have enough humanitarian reasons, the officer may issue your permanent residency. Keep in mind, the following issues.

- H&C applications are for Canadian permanent residency.
- They highly depend on the judgement of a trained officer. The refusal rate on these applications is very high.
- Your humanitarian reasons need to overcome any inadmissibility or lack of requirements issues.
- If the inadmissibility is because of security, human rights violations, or organized criminality, the H&C application is not an option.

H&C FACTORS

When you submit an H&C application, the officer considers the following factors, before deciding.

- What are the best interests of the minor children who are affected by the decision?

- Can the country of the applicant provide the healthcare services they need?
- What are the ties of the applicant to Canada and how established are they in our country?
- Will they face family violence if they go back to their home country?
- What is the potential hardship they face if they go back to their home country?
- Are there any negative consequences for the relatives due to their separation?
- How difficult is it for them to leave Canada?
- Are they able to establish their lives in Canada?
- Is there any specific factor that justifies the issuance of permanent residency?

Keep in mind that this list is only a guideline. An officer may look into many other factors to decide. The officers heavily rely on the documents you provide. However, they may also conduct their research.

Remember, if you present issues that characterize you as a refuge, then the officer may refuse your H&C request. Consult with a professional to make sure you are not a refugee.

TWO DIFFERENT TYPES OF H&C APPLICATIONS

There are two different ways to submit a Humanitarian and Compassionate Grounds Application.

1. You may submit a regular application package to the immigration authorities, but you include all H&C documents in the package. Make sure to mention you are requesting an exemption under the H&C grounds.
2. If you are already in Canada, then you may prepare a standalone H&C application and then submit it to the local processing centre responsible for such applications. The current processing centre responsible for H&C cases is in Vancouver, British Columbia.

Due to the complexities of H&C cases, you need to consult with an immigration professional. Do not do it yourself!

TWO STAGES OF AN IN-CANADA H&C APPLICATION

If you submit your application in Canada, the officer reviews the application and then either refuses your request or approves the H&C elements of it. If they approve the H&C elements or rather you pass the stage one, then you may request the following:

- **A stay of the removal order** – If you have received a removal order, you may now ask the officer to put the removal order on hold till they finalize the processing of your application.
- **A work permit** – You may now request an open work permit.

The second stage of the processing includes medical examinations and background check for potential inadmissibility. Of course, the background check does not include those elements that the officer ignores because of H&C grounds. For example, if someone is inadmissible because of criminality, then the officer does not include criminality in the background check, but they consider the other eight grounds of inadmissibility.

H&C FOR OTHER SITUATIONS

Sometimes permanent residents of Canada lose their permanent residency because they did not stay in Canada enough. In these situations, they may request to keep their permanent residency based on humanitarian and compassionate considerations.

While H&C does not apply to temporary applications such as TRV, eTA, work permit, or study permit, you may include those elements in your application. The officers have no mandate to accept H&C for temporary applications though.

ALTERNATIVES TO H&C

Depending on the specifics of your application, you sometimes may try alternative options such as,

- Receiving a record suspension (pardon) for criminal history in Canada
- Asking for rehabilitation for criminal history outside Canada

- Requesting a Temporary Resident Permit (see Tip # 79)
- Claiming refugee status in Canada (see Tip # 46)
- Applying for a Declaration of Relief under subsection 42.1(1) of the IRPA for inadmissibility to Canada under section 34 (security), paragraphs 35(1)(b) or (c) (human or international rights violations), and/or subsection 37(1) (organized criminality) of the IRPA
- In the case of inadmissibility due to misrepresentation, waiting for five years and then apply
- Finding alternative immigration options under which you meet all the requirements

PART THREE:
WORKING IN CANADA

TIP # 48: WORK IN CANADA WITHOUT A PERMIT, LEGALLY!

Thomas is an Australian vocalist and actor. He has appeared on many live musicals in Australia, Japan, and Malaysia. He currently performs as the lead actor for a musical that will tour Europe and North America. As part of their tour, they will perform in four Canadian cities of Calgary, Halifax, Thunder Bay, and Winnipeg. Thomas will stay in Canada for about four weeks while they travel from one city to the other. The Australian company will take care of his salary, accommodation, and transportation. Thomas is wondering if he needs to get a work permit to be able to perform in Canada.

Most foreign nationals who intend to work in Canada need work permits, but under certain circumstances, foreign workers may work in Canada without a permit.

WHO COULD WORK IN CANADA WITHOUT A WORK PERMIT?

Section 186 of the Immigration and Refugee Protection Regulations (IRPR) lists all potential options for working in Canada without a work permit. The following list loosely shows those options.

1. Business visitors
2. Foreign diplomats or employees of foreign governments if approved by Global Affairs Canada
3. The family members of group # 2
4. Members of visiting armed forces
5. Officers of foreign countries exchanged with Canadians to work for the federal or provincial governments of Canada
6. Maritime law enforcement officers of the United States
7. In-flight security officers
8. Performing artists as solo performers or members of larger groups
9. Key members of performing arts groups
10. Participants in sports activities or events
11. Journalists
12. Speakers such as keynote speakers or paid speakers
13. Organizers of certain conventions or events
14. Certain spiritual leaders or workers
15. Judges of sports competitions or artistic events
16. Evaluators or examiners of research proposals or academic projects, etc.
17. Expert witnesses for courts or the governments
18. Certain healthcare students
19. Aviation inspectors
20. Aviation incidents investigators
21. Flight crews
22. Emergency personnel to deal with disasters
23. Post-secondary international students who hold valid study permits and studying at designated learning institutions, if they work 20 hours or less per week
24. International students who have completed their studies and

have applied for a Post-graduate Work Permit (PGWP), but they have not received a decision on their work permit yet

This list does not show the conditions attached to each group. You may consult with an immigration professional for more information. Generally speaking, consider the following:

- The work must be limited to the nature of exemption. For example, healthcare students will work at a hospital or healthcare centre to enhance their skills.

- There might be time limitations. For example, the event a speaker attends needs to be five days or less.

- The source of remuneration in many cases is a foreign entity. For example, performing artists are paid by their foreign employer in most cases (exceptions apply).

HOW CAN A FOREIGN NATIONAL ENTER CANADA FOR THESE TYPES OF WORK?

The regular rules of entering Canada applies to these foreign nationals. For example, if they are from a visa exempt country, they usually need to apply for an eTA (the US citizens are exempt from eTA). If they need a visa, then they have to apply for a TRV. If they are inadmissible to Canada, they need to apply for a TRP, Rehabilitation, or an Authorization to Return to Canada (ARC), depending on the issues surrounding their inadmissibility.

When you are applying for entry, make sure to present enough documentation to show the reason you intend to visit Canada and why you are exempt from a work permit. Bring those documents with you to the port of entry.

TIP # 49: LMIA PROCESS AND TYPES

Lethabo is a senior risk analyst at a famous company in Soweto, South Africa. Lethabo masters English and German languages. He has more than ten years of experience in the field. Lethabo holds an MBA in Financing and two certificates in the field of risk management from two renowned institutions in Germany and the United States. A financial institution in Canada has recently offered Lethabo a senior risk analyst position at their company's headquarters in Edmonton, Alberta. They know they have to get an LMIA before initiating the work permit application, but they do not know where to start, the fees involved, and the process of an LMIA application.

LMIA stands for Labour Market Impact Assessment. When an employer receives a positive LMIA, it means they may hire a foreign worker for the position they are offering without negatively impacting the Canadian labour market. It is good to know, the organization that develops LMIA process and reviews LMIA applications is the Employment and Social Skills Development Canada (ESDC) also known as Service Canada. The LMIA former name was LMO or Labour Market Opinion.

TYPES OF LMIA

Interestingly, LMIA comes into different types. ESDC in consultation with IRCC decides on the types of LMIA. We can currently identify the following types of LMIA.

- **LMIA for permanent residency (PR)**: If you are applying for immigration to Canada and you receive a positive LMIA, you may enhance your chances of getting approved (especially under the Express Entry system). Generally speaking, the PR LMIA is the easiest kind of LMIA as the applicant will enter the job market only if they become permanent residents of Canada. The processing fee of a pure LMIA for Permanent Residency is CAD 0.00 at the moment. See also Tip # 28 for more information on job offers for immigration to Canada.

- **LMIA for Global Talent Stream**: This LMIA targets certain positions (mostly in the IT sector) that demand highly talented individuals. The salary must also be high (usually CAD 80,000 per year or more). If your position falls under this stream, the government will process your application fairly quickly.

- **LMIA for high-wage positions**: If the Canadian employer offers a job to the applicant and the salary is equal or higher than the median salary of that position in their province, they need to apply for a High-wage LMIA.

- **LMIA for low-wage positions**: If the salary is below the median wage of the province, the job is a low-wage job. Getting an LMIA for these kinds of positions is extremely difficult.

- **LMIA for agricultural workers**: ESDC issues LMIA for agricultural workers under two major programs, namely: Seasonal Agricultural Worker Program (SAWP) and Agricultural Stream.

- **LMIA for in-home caregivers**: This type of LMIA is for those in-home caregivers that take care of minor children, elderly persons who are 65 or older, and people with disabilities or serious chronic or terminal illnesses. The government of Canada intends to make changes to the caregiver program. Consequently, they may change the process and conditions for this type of LMIA.

LMIA PROCESS

Depending on the type of LMIA, you may need to take some or all of these steps to apply for an LMIA to ESDC and eventually get a work permit:

- **Try to hire local employees and show the Canadian employer have failed to succeed**: Recruitment efforts could include advertising on job search websites, local media, internal hiring, approaching underrepresented groups such as people with disabilities, vulnerable youths, newcomers, or indigenous people. The employer also needs to review the resumes of local applicants and invite them to job interviews. The minimum duration of the hiring efforts is usually four weeks.

- **Prepare documents and submit them to ESDC**: The documents could include proof of recruitment, business legitimacy (i.e. the business is active and capable of paying the salary of the foreign national), transition plan or labour market benefits plan, employment contract, LMIA application forms, etc.

- **Pay the processing fee and apply to ESDC**: The processing fee for most applications is CAD 1000, but some exceptions may apply (e.g. the processing fee for permanent residence LMIA is $0.00 if the foreign national does not intend to work for the employer before becoming a permanent resident of Canada)

- **Review by an ESDC officer**: An ESDC officer reviews the application. They may accept or refuse the application immediately, but in many cases, they call the employer and ask more questions or request more documents before finalizing their decision.

- **Submit the Work Permit application**: If ESDC issues a positive LMIA, you need to apply to the immigration authorities to receive the Work Permit.

TIP # 50: WORK IN CANADA WITHOUT AN LMIA

Chloe is a citizen of France. She holds a bachelor's degree in communication and more than five years of work experience as a public relations coordinator for Peugeot Motocycles in Mandeure, France. A Canadian company in Winnipeg, Manitoba has recently offered Chloe a position as their French public relations manager. She is extremely excited about the offer and wonders if she can move to Canada quickly and work for the Canadian company.

Foreign nationals who intend to work in Canada, usually need a positive LMIA from the Employment and Social Development Canada for their position. The purpose of LMIA or rather the Labour Market Impact Assessment is to make sure the employment of the foreign national does not affect the Canadian job market negatively (see Tip # 49).

The process of LMIA is time-consuming and expensive. That's why many candidates and employers look for potential options that exempt them from it. The IRCC exempt some jobs or foreign nationals from LMIA under a special program called the *International Mobility Program* or IMP.

IMP exemptions are because of the international agreements Canada signs with other countries, the Canadian interests, or other reasons. We can divide IMP into five major groups:

- International agreements
- Canadian interests
- No other means of support
- Permanent residence applicants in Canada
- Humanitarian reasons[17]

INTERNATIONAL AGREEMENTS

Canada signs many agreements with other countries. As part of some of those agreements, Canada and the other signatories ease up the labour movement process for their citizens. Some of the existing agreements that exempt certain foreign nationals from an LMIA include,

- Non-trade, including but not limited to,
    - Airline Telecommunication & Information Services (SITA) – A special agreement that affects a Montreal-based company
    - Canada-Bermuda Memorandum of Understanding, Professional Trainees
    - Canada-U.S. Understanding of Arrangement – This one is for the US IRS employees
    - Cooperative Waterfowl Survey & Banding Program – A program between the United States Fish and Wildlife Service and the Canadian Wildlife Service
    - International Air Transport Association (IATA)
    - Jamaica: Seasonal Agricultural Program, Liaison Officers
    - Malaysia, Professional Accounting Trainees
    - North Atlantic Treaty Organization (NATO)
    - Organization for Economic Co-operation & Development (OECD)
    - U.S. Government Personnel
- North American Free Trade Agreement (NAFTA) – Soon to become the United States-Mexico-Canada treaty (USMCA) – See Tip # 56

- Free Trade Agreements (FTA) with some countries, such as
    - Canada-Chile FTA
    - Canada-Peru FTA
    - Canada-Colombia FTA
    - Canada-Korea FTA
    - Canada–Panama FTA
- Canada-European Union Comprehensive Economic and Trade Agreement (CETA)
- General Agreement on Trade in Services (GATS)
- Comprehensive and Progressive Agreement for Trans-Pacific Partnership (CPTPP)

This list could change at any time. The terms and conditions under each agreement are different. For example, many of these agreements support intra-company transferees. If a company has a branch both in Canada and the other country, foreign employees may work in Canada without an LMIA. Of course, some agreements are a lot more comprehensive. Some of them do not offer this option at all. You need to visit the IRCC website or consult with a professional for your potential options.

CANADIAN INTERESTS

Sometimes it is in the best interest of Canada to accept a foreign employee without an LMIA. Imagine an entrepreneur that invests in Canada and creates jobs for Canadians. In such situations, the IRCC does not expect an LMIA. Some existing examples of Canadian Interests include the following:

- Significant benefit – Sometimes hiring a foreign national could have significant benefits for Canada. For example, hiring a celebrity athlete or a coach.
- Entrepreneurs and self-employed people – For more information about this option see Tip # 35
- Emergency repairs or repair personnel for out-of-warranty equipment
- Television and film production workers (see Tip # 57)
- Francophone mobility (see Tip # 53)

- Bridging open work permits for some people who are already in Canada and have applied for permanent residency
- Reciprocal employment – For example the NHL players. Some Americans work in Canada as professional Hockey players, but in return, some Canadians work in the United States
- Youth exchange programs – This option covers some countries such as some European Union members, South Korea, and Japan
- Performing arts (see Tip # 59)
- Spouses of skilled workers and international students
- Charitable or religious work

Some members of this group may work in Canada for any employers, but the majority of the candidates under this category need to find an employer first.

NO OTHER MEANS OF SUPPORT

This option covers two groups of people only, namely:

- Refugee claimants or rather people who have filed a refugee claim but have not received a decision on their claim yet
- Persons who are under an unenforceable removal order (See Tip # 73 for more information about removal orders)

If IRCC issues a work permit for these people, the permit will be open. It means the applicant may work for any employer in Canada, subject to certain restrictions.

PERMANENT RESIDENCE APPLICANTS IN CANADA

Some people may apply for permanent residency from inside Canada. If you are a member of any of the following groups, you may apply for a work permit without an LMIA or even an employer.

- Caregiver or live-in-caregiver class
- Spouse or common-law partner in Canada class
- Protected persons or rather people who have received a positive

decision on their refugee claim but have not received their permanent residency yet.

- People who have received an initial positive decision on their H&C application (see Tip # 47)
- Family members of the above

The work permits for this group is also open to any employer subject to certain restrictions.

HUMANITARIAN REASONS

The last IMP option covers the following groups:

- Destitute international students. This group refers to those international students that because of unforeseen sudden changes to their lives cannot pay for their expenses. Examples could include the death of their parents, an internal war in their home country, or an earthquake that destroys their hometown.
- Holders of a temporary resident permit (TRP) valid for a minimum of six months (see Tip # 79 for more information on TRP)

The work permits for this group is open and subject to certain restriction.

HOW TO APPLY FOR A WORK PERMIT WITHOUT AN LMIA?

There is no simple answer to this question. Your best bet is to consult with a professional immigration lawyer or consultant. They will assess your situation to find out if your job requires an LMIA or could be exempt from it.

---

[17] Source: https://www.canada.ca/en/immigration-refugees-citizenship/corporate/publications-manuals/operational-bulletins-manuals/temporary-residents/foreign-workers/exemption-codes.html

TIP # 51: THREE STEPS TO WORK IN CANADA

Verrill is a professional welder from Costa Rica. He has more than eight years of experience as a welder. Verrill speaks English to the extent that he can communicate well and understand instructions. He has heard there are many job opportunities for welders in Canada. Verrill wonders if he can work in Canada and if the answer is yes what steps he needs to take.

Canada is one of the top ten economies on earth. Many people in the world love to work and live in Canada. Our country welcomes more than 250,000 foreign workers every year. They work in different sectors such as agriculture, IT, manufacturing, natural resources, etc. Some of the workers are researchers or highly skilled workers, and some of them are low skilled workers or anywhere in between. Some stay in Canada for a few weeks and some for a few years. If you want to be one of those foreign workers, you generally need to take the following three steps.

- Step One – Get a job offer
- Step Two – Get the preliminary documents
- Step Three – Get a Work Permit

STEP ONE – GET A JOB OFFER

To get a job offer, you need a valid Canadian employer. Some people find these employers via family or friends or even government-run programs such as the Seasonal Agricultural Worker Program or SAWP. If you do not have access to any of those services, you may consider approaching Canadian recruitment agencies or Canadian career websites. The chances of getting a job offer via the websites are low, but it's not a bad idea if you upload your resume and hope for the best. The following list is not comprehensive but could help you start your search.

- jobbank.gc.ca
- indeed.ca
- monster.ca
- workopolis.com

If you are a US citizen or hold a valid visit visa to Canada or if you may travel to Canada with an eTA, then you may also consider visiting our country first and talk to the potential employers in person. Whatever you do, remember that nobody is allowed to charge you a fee to find you jobs in Canada. The practice is illegal.

Read the following Tips for more information about job hunting techniques:

- Tip # 55: Cold Calling for Job Search
- Tip # 54: Job Search Websites
- Tip # 86: Sample Canadian Resumes

STEP TWO – GET THE PRELIMINARY DOCUMENTS

The Canadian employer usually needs to get a special permit from the Canadian labour office or rather the ESDC (the Employment and Social Development Canada). They call this permit the Labour Market Impact Assessment (LMIA). If the employer receives a positive LMIA you may proceed with the Work Permit application (see Tip # 49).

Sometimes the position you apply for is exempt from an LMIA (see Tip # 50). In these situations, the employer usually needs to apply for an exemption code via their employer account on the IRCC (Immigration,

Refugees, and Citizenship Canada) website.

While the employer applies for an LMIA or an LMIA exemption code, you also need to prepare certain documents such as identification documents, work permit forms, and documents that show you meet the requirements of the job.

STEP THREE – GET A WORK PERMIT

Some jobs are exempt from a Work Permit (e.g. a speaker of an event that is five days or less or an athlete who participates in a game in Canada. See Tip # 48 for more information). Majority of jobs in Canada, however, require a Work Permit. The Work Permit allows you to stay and work in Canada.

If you pass the first two steps successfully, you need to apply for a Work Permit. Every applicant may apply for a Work Permit to a Canadian Visa Office outside Canada.

If you are exempt from a visit visa or the purpose of travelling to Canada, then you could apply for the Work Permit at a Port of Entry. Some individuals may even apply for their Work Permit after entering Canada. Consult with a professional for your options.

A Work Permit could be valid for a few days to a few years. It may impose certain limitations though (e.g. the position, the employer, and the location). Make sure to comply with all the requirements of the Work Permit to avoid losing it or deportation from Canada.

If you have a family (spouse or children), they could also accompany you to Canada under certain circumstances. Consult with a professional for more information.

Keep in mind that a Work Permit is temporary. If you intend to live in Canada permanently, then you need to consider immigrating to Canada (see Tip # 4 for a list of options).

TIP # 52: WORK PERMIT AND IMMIGRATION OPTIONS FOR ARTISTS

Sasha is a Russian ballerina. Although she is only 28, she has been professionally active for more than 12 years. She has appeared on many national and world stages. Sasha has travelled to several countries in the past to perform as an acclaimed dancer. A Canadian ballet company has offered Sasha a permanent position. She wonders if she may work for the Canadian company and eventually become a permanent resident of Canada.

Canadian government offers many work permit and immigration options to foreign applicants. Some of these options are open to the majority of the applicants, but some are limited to a specific group. Luckily, there are many opportunities for artists (especially performing artists) to either work or immigrate to Canada.

WORKING IN CANADA WITHOUT A PERMIT

Sometimes performing artists or some other people who are involved with cultural activities may work in Canada without a work permit. Here is a brief list of those options. Of course, you need to consult with a professional to make sure you fall under any of these categories.

- Artists who work in Canada in the capacity of a business visitor [note to practitioners – see R186(a)]
- A performing artist appearing alone or in a group in artistic performance or a member of the staff integral to the artistic performance,
  - In a foreign production or as guests of Canadian production, and
  - If no employment relationship with the Canadian company exists [note to practitioners – see R186(g)]
- Speakers [note to practitioners – see R186(j)]
- Judges of artistic events [note to practitioners – see R186(m)]

See Tip # 48 for more details on working in Canada without a permit.

If a person qualifies for working without a permit, they still need to make one of the following applications before entering Canada.

- Temporary Resident Visa (TRV), for those who are not exempt from a visa to enter Canada
- Electronic Travel Authorization (eTA), for those who are exempt from a TRV
- Application for Rehabilitation, for those who have committed criminal offences outside Canada a long time ago (usually more than five years ago), and they need to clear their names before entering Canada
- Application for Record Suspension (pardon), for those who have committed criminal offences inside Canada a long time ago, and they need to clear their names before entering Canada
- Temporary Resident Permit (TRP), for those who are inadmissible to Canada and do not qualify for Record Suspension or Rehabilitation

US citizens and some other people are exempt from both eTA or TRV, but if they have inadmissibility issues, they may need to apply for Rehabilitation, Record Suspension (pardon), or TRP, depending on their circumstances. Regardless, they need to make sure to present enough documentation at the port of entry to show why they are visiting Canada and why they are exempt from a Work Permit (e.g. business visitors may need to present a business invitation letter among other documents).

WORKING IN CANADA WITH AN LMIA

If you intend to work in Canada, you often need to get a certificate called LMIA from an ESDC officer (see Tip # 49). The LMIA process is complex, time-consuming, and expensive. However, some artistic jobs require LMIA. For example, if a music school hires a foreign music teacher, they normally need to apply for an LMIA first. If they receive a positive LMIA, they may apply for a work permit. Of course, under certain circumstances, working without an LMIA is possible. The following section lists some of those situations.

WORKING IN CANADA WITHOUT AN LMIA

The International Mobility Program (IMP) makes working without an LMIA possible (see Tip # 50). This program focuses on the international agreements Canada signs with other countries, the Canadian interests, or humanitarian reasons. The following list shows some LMIA exemption options available to artists.

- Tip # 57: TV and film production
- Tip # 58: Significant contributions to Canada
- Tip # 59: Reciprocity for performing artists
- Tip # 53: Francophone mobility
- Tip # 35: Self-employed or entrepreneurs

The applicant may be exempt under many other options (e.g. under USMCA, bridging work permits, accompanying a family member who is an international student or foreign worker, etc.).

LMIA exemption does not exempt a person from a work permit. If you are exempt from an LMIA, you still need to apply for a work permit.

IMMIGRATION TO CANADA

If you immigrate to Canada, you will become a permanent resident of Canada and eventually a naturalized citizen. While there are many options available to artists, the following options pop up most of the time:

- Tip # 32: Federal Self-employed program
    - International artists stream
    - Self-employed artists stream
- Tip # 22: Express Entry
    - Tip # 23 and 24: Federal Skilled Worker Program
    - Tip # 25: Canadian Experience Class

Some artists could apply under other streams of immigration (e.g. start-up visa or PNP).

TIP # 53: WORK PERMIT FOR FRANCOPHONES

Florent is a business coordinator for a textile manufacturer in Cameroon. Being a Francophone person, he likes to move to Canada and work there. Florent knows that Quebec is the only francophone province in Canada. However, he prefers to stay in Windsor, Ontario. He knows a couple of friends there and loves to stay close to the Francophone community in LaSalle. Florent wonders if he could make this happen.

Canada has two official languages: French and English. According to Statistics Canada, the primary language of about 65% of Canadians is English, about 21% is French, and the rest speak unofficial languages. Of course, many people know both official languages of Canada[18].

Paragraph 3(1)(b.1) of the Immigration and Refugee Protection Act (IRPA) defines supporting and assisting "the development of minority official languages communities in Canada" as one of the objectives of the IRPA. About 89% of French-speaking people (also known as Francophones) live in the province of Quebec[19]. The rest of Canada is mainly English speaking (also known as Anglophones). It is clear that the Francophone population is a minority in other provinces. The total population of French-speaking people is hardly over 1,000,000 outside Quebec[20]. If you compare these statistics with the mandate of IRPA, you realize why the

The government of Canada wishes to invite Francophones to other provinces of Canada.

WHO IS A FRANCOPHONE?

The governing body of Canadian immigration is the Immigration, Refugees, and Citizenship Canada (IRCC). Under the IRCC guidelines, a Francophone is someone whose habitual language of daily use is French. The obvious choices are many people from the following countries:

Algeria	Djibouti	Mauritius
Belgium	Equatorial Guinn	Monaco
Benin	France	Morocco
Burkina Faso	French Guiana	Niger
Burundi	Gabon	Réunion
Cameroon	Guadeloupe	Rwanda
Central African Republic	Guinea	Senegal
Chad	Haiti	Seychelles
Comoros	Luxembourg	Switzerland
Congo, Republic of the	Madagascar	Togo
Côte d'Ivoire	Mali	Tunisia
The Democratic Republic of the Congo	Martinique	

The official language of the preceding countries is French, and many people from those countries fall under the definition of Francophone (assuming they use French as their primary language in daily life). If a person is from other countries, they may still apply. However, they need to show they use French daily. Some examples include a person who is a French language teacher or someone who works for the Embassy of France or Belgium in their home country. An immigration officer has the right to ask for proof of knowledge of French language (e.g. through the Test d'évaluation de français pour le Canada score).

WORK PERMIT FOR FRANCOPHONES

French-speaking people could receive a work permit to Canada under the Mobilité francophone (or Francophone Mobility) program. The applicants under this program are exempt from an LMIA. To qualify for this program, you need to.

- Be a Francophone as described earlier
- Your destination is a province in Canada other than Quebec
- You have a job offer from a Canadian employer under NOC 0, A or B (see Tip # 16)
- Your knowledge of French language in Niveaux de compétence Linguistique canadiens (NCLC) is of level 7 or higher (NCLC is the Canadian Language Benchmark for French)

As mentioned earlier the officer may or may not ask you for proof of knowledge in French, but if they do, they will most likely ask for the TEF Canada or TCF Canada exams scores. The following table shows the minimum scores under each ability for each exam.

Test	Speaking	Listening	Reading	Writing
TEF Canada	310	249	207	310
TCF Canada	10	458	453	10

Remember these are minimums. If the officer asks for the test results, you'd better offer higher scores.

STEPS TO BE TAKEN

To apply under this program, you and your employer need to take the following steps.

1. An employer needs to offer you a full-time job outside Quebec in a NOC 0, A, or B position.
2. If you accept the offer, the employer needs to create an Employer Account with the IRCC and post the job over there. They also need to pay the compliance fee of $230.
3. Upon posting the job offer, you will receive a special file number

that starts with letter A. You need to apply for a Work Permit with the help of that job offer.

Since Francophone Mobility is considered an outside Canada application, you are better to apply online before entering Canada. Consult with a professional for more information.

WHAT HAPPENS TO THE FAMILY MEMBERS?

If you have a spouse or children, they may also move to Canada with you. Your spouse or common-law partner could receive an open work permit which allows them to work for any employer. Your minor children may receive a visitor record, which allow them to study in Canada. Many factors affect the potential options for your spouse and your children.

IMMIGRATION OPTIONS

Francophone mobility could open doors to immigration to Canada under the Express Entry system. For example, if you work for your employer for at least one year in Canada, you collect extra points which in turn makes it easier for you to apply. Your chances to succeed depend on many factors such as your age, your knowledge of French or English, your work experience, your ties to Canada, admissibility to Canada, and more.

---

[18] https://www12.statcan.gc.ca/census-recensement/2011/dp-pd/hlt-fst/lang/Pages/Highlight.cfm?TabID=1&Lang=E&PRCode=01&Age=1&tableID=403&queryID=1

[19] https://en.wikipedia.org/wiki/French_language_in_Canada

[20] https://en.wikipedia.org/wiki/French_language_in_Canada

TIP # 54: JOB SEARCH WEBSITES

Abbud is a citizen of Qatar. He intends to work in Canada, but he has no friends or relatives there. Abbud knows English very well. He is hoping to be able to find a job offer with the help of the internet.

If you intend to work in Canada, you need to get a job offer first. In other words, a Canadian employer needs to offer you a position in their company, and then you may move forward with the work permit process (see Tip # 51). There are many ways to seek jobs in Canada, and one of them is looking for jobs via Canadian job search websites.

The following lists help you locate many of those websites. Of course, you need to prepare a good resume and cover letter before any job search efforts (see Tip # 86). Job search websites are also known as job boards and career search websites. The following lists are not a measure for comparing these websites. They simply show your options for an online job search in Canada.

FEDERAL JOB SEARCH WEBSITES

These websites post jobs about any potential location in Canada. Our country has ten provinces and three territories. The following websites could post jobs for any of those provinces or territories.

- **jobbank.gc.ca** – This website belongs to the Federal

Government of Canada. Every employer who wants to hire an employee from outside Canada must post jobs on this website. It is a busy website.

- **indeed.ca** – I hire most of our employees via this website. As an employer, we have found this website to be the most effective one. Consider posting your resume on this website and constantly look for potential career opportunities.

- **monster.ca** – This website is present all over the world under different domain names. It is active in Canada under the name of monster.ca.

- **workopolis.com** – When I immigrated to Canada, this website was the main website for job search. It is still very famous but very expensive for many employers to post their jobs.

- **allstarjobs.ca** – This website allows to search for jobs in several cities of Canada.

- **elute.ca** – I am not familiar with this website, but you may give it a try.

- **kijiji.ca** – This website posts jobs among many other items. You need to be specific about the location you want to work. Be careful as many scammers post jobs on this website.

- **craigslist.ca** – Craigslist is a classified ads website. You need to pick your city first and then look for this website on google. Just like Kijiji.ca watch for scammers on craigslist.ca.

PROVINCIAL WEBSITES

Federal career search websites post jobs for most of Canada. Some job boards focus on specific provinces. The following list shows some of those websites. The numbers next to each province represent the approximate population based on the 2016 national census. I have also included the name of the capital of each province or territory for guidance. The second city, if shown, refers to the most populated city in the province.

- British Columbia (4,650,000 – Victoria, Vancouver): bcjobs.ca, workbc.ca

- Alberta (4,000,000 – Edmonton, Calgary): albertajobcentre.ca, calgaryjobboard.ca

- Saskatchewan (1,100,000 – Regina, Saskatoon): saskjobs.ca

- Manitoba (1,280,000 – Winnipeg): mbjobs.ca

- Ontario (13,450,000 – Toronto): I couldn't locate any websites dedicated to Ontario, but you may use the Federal websites for this province. You may also visit gojobs.gov.on.ca, but the jobs posted on this website are related to the Government of Ontario. These kinds of jobs are usually not available to foreign nationals.

- Quebec (8,170,000 – Quebec City, Montreal): jobboom.com

- New Brunswick (750,000 – Fredericton, Moncton): nbjobs.ca

- Nova Scotia (924,000 – Halifax): novascotiajobshop.ca

- Prince Edward Island (143,000 – Charlottetown): employmentjourney.com

- Newfoundland and Labrador (520,000 – St. John's): newfoundlandandlabradorjobshop.ca

- Yukon (36,000 – Whitehorse): yukongovernment.hua.hrsmart.com

- Northwest Territories (42,000 – Yellowknife): gov.nt.ca/careers

- Nunavut (36,000 – Iqaluit): I could only locate a website for government jobs.

Consider these lists as guidelines only. Feel free to find other potential websites with the help of Google.

TIP # 55: COLD CALLING FOR JOB SEARCH

Hekla is a human resource professional from Iceland. She masters both English and French languages. Hekla holds an MBA. She has more than eight years of experience in the field of human resources. Hekla is currently in Toronto to visit an old friend. She intends to stay in Canada for one month. While here, Hekla intends to find a job opportunity and move to Canada as a temporary foreign worker.

Foreign workers usually live outside Canada, and their potential job search opportunities are normally limited to job search websites or family or friends who live in Canada. Both options offer little success rate. If you are in Canada, you may consider another option: cold calling.

I hired one of our team members because of cold-calling a couple of years ago. A job seeker left his resume in our office. I reviewed the resume and liked it. We didn't have an opening at the time. Regardless, I invited him to an interview. We offered him a position a few weeks later when an opening became available.

WHAT IS COLD CALLING IN JOB HUNT?

Canadian employers usually post their openings on job boards (see Tip # 54). However, many of them eventually hire someone who they know. One way to make yourself known to an employer is to meet them or call them. There are two ways you may do this:

- Visit the employer's office in person
- Call them on the phone

Both options are cold calling.

VISITING THE EMPLOYER'S OFFICE

If you intend to visit the employer's office in person, consider the following:

1. Visit the employer's website and familiarize yourself with their business as much as you can.
2. Try to prepare a well-written résumé (see Tip # 86). Make sure the résumé is truthful, yet it relates to the employer.
3. If there is a specific opening in the company that matches your skills or expertise, study it carefully and know every aspect of it.
4. Do your best to find out the names and roles of potential decision-makers. You may get help from LinkedIn or the employer's website.
5. Based on the research you have done about the employer and the potential job opening, prepare answers to some potential questions (e.g. your experience and how it matches the job)
6. Prepare some questions to ask from the employer. Those questions show you understand the employer well and willing to work for them.
7. While you are visiting the employer's office, make sure to "dress to impress." In other words, be business-like and well groomed.
8. Be ready for rejection. Some employers are quite receptive, and they may even invite you to an interview on the spot. Some of them may arrange for an interview in the future. Some employers may collect your resume, and some may even refuse to accept the resume from you. Get yourself mentally ready for any scenario. Regardless of the employer's reaction maintain a professional attitude.

The larger the employer, the less likely you will be able to get in touch with a decision-maker. I believe the cold-calling option works for medium size or small businesses, but you may give large businesses a try.

MAKING PHONE CALLS TO EMPLOYERS

Calling the employers is not as effective as visiting them in person, but it has some advantages. For example, you may call several employers in a single day, and you do not need to spend money on the commute to their location. You may also reach out to those employers that are in other parts of Canada. If you plan to make phone calls to the employers, you need to consider items 1 to 6 on the list I posted for visiting employers. Also, get ready for more rejections.

SPECIAL CONSIDERATIONS FOR FOREIGN WORKERS

When you are hunting for jobs in Canada, consider the following:

- Most of the job offers need the approval of the ESDC (Employment and Social Development Canada). You need to receive a positive LMIA before you initiate the work permit process for most of the jobs (see Tip #49). The LMIA process is time-consuming and costly. The employer is responsible for those expenses. Consequently, make sure of the following:

    o The employer needs to be an active business for a few years and have some full-time employees

    o The employer should not be on the blacklist of the ESDC.

    o The employer needs to be ready to cover all the necessary expenses for you. The extent of the employer's commitment depends on the salary they offer to you in comparison to the median salary offered to a Canadian or permanent resident of Canada.

- As a foreign worker, you have similar rights to citizens or permanent resident workers.

- A good read: Take these 3 Steps to Work in Canada (Tip # 51)

TIP # 56: USMCA (NAFTA 2.0)

Noah, a US citizen, is a successful IT professional. He currently works as an IT department manager for a large American corporation. Noah's company intends to transfer him to their new branch in St. John's in Newfoundland and Labrador for six months. He knows, he needs a work permit, and his company is taking care of the process. Noah is, however, curious about the process and the type of work permit he is going to receive.

The all-new USMCA agreement or rather the United States – Mexico – Canada trade agreement will replace the old North Atlantic Free Trade Agreement (NAFTA). While USMCA affects many aspects of trade interactions between the three countries, it also deals with the matter of visa and work permits for the citizens of these countries. Chapter 16 of the USMCA discusses the following four groups of people.

- Business Visitors (Section A – Annex 1603)
- Traders and Investors (Section B – Annex 1603)
- Intra-company Transferees (Section C – Annex 1603)
- Professionals (Section D – Annex 1603)

This tip views USMCA from the Canadian visa and work-permit point of view. You may see Tip # 50 first for more information about working in

Canada without an LMIA.

The IRCC has not released the LMIA exempt codes for USMCA as of now. That's why portions of this tip reflect NAFTA rather than USMCA. I have taken some portions of this tip from Chapter 16 of the USMCA verbatim.

The term Party, in this tip, means either the US, Mexico, or Canada. The USMCA agreement affects the citizens of these countries only. It does not affect the permanent residents of these countries.

BUSINESS VISITORS (SECTION A – ANNEX 1603)

Under Article 1601, a "business person means a citizen of a Party who is engaged in trade in goods, the provision of services or the conduct of investment activities." Further to this definition, section 187 of the Immigration and Refugee Protection Regulations of Canada (IRPR) defines a business visitor as a foreign national "who seeks to engage in international business activities in Canada without directly entering the Canadian labour market." It further categorizes the business visitors to the following groups:

- foreign nationals purchasing Canadian goods or services for a foreign business or government, or receiving training or familiarization in respect of such goods or services;

- foreign nationals receiving or giving training within a Canadian parent or subsidiary of the corporation that employs them outside Canada, if any production of goods or services that results from the training is incidental; and

- foreign nationals representing a foreign business or government for the purpose of selling goods for that business or government, if the foreign national is not engaged in making sales to the general public in Canada.

Subsection 187(3) of the IRPA emphasizes the activities must meet the following conditions.

a) the primary source of remuneration for the business activities is outside Canada; and

b) the principal place of business and actual place of accrual of profits remain predominately outside Canada.

Under Section A – Annex 1603 of the USMCA, business visitors who are citizens of the United States or Mexico may enter Canada and engage in business activities without authorization. In other words, they do not need a work permit to work in Canada. While this privilege extends to other nationalities under section 186 of the IRPR, the USMCA re-emphasizes the matter for the US and Mexican citizens.

The US business visitors may enter Canada without a visa or an eTA. They only need to have proper documents with them to show to a Border Services Officer their intention to visit and stay in Canada.

The Mexican business visitors need to obtain an eTA before flying to Canada. If they are entering Canada at a seaport or land crossing, they do not need an eTA. However, I highly recommend it.

If the business visitor, regardless of their nationality, has a criminal history, they need to contact an immigration professional for advice as they could be inadmissible to Canada.

TRADERS AND INVESTORS (SECTION B – ANNEX 1603)

Under Section B – Annex 1603, US and Mexican citizens are considered traders or investors if their purpose of the visit is:

a) carry on substantial trade in goods or services principally between the territory of the Party of which the business person is a citizen and the territory of the Party into which entry is sought, or

b) establish, develop, administer or provide advice or key technical services to the operation of an investment to which the business person or the business person's enterprise has committed, or is in the process of committing, a substantial amount of capital

Under the old NAFA rules, Traders and Investors are not exempt from a work permit, but they may receive their work permit without an LMIA under subsection 204 of the IRPR (the old codes T21 and T22 respectively). I suspect, the same policy will be followed by the IRCC under the new USMCA.

INTRA-COMPANY TRANSFEREES (SECTION C – ANNEX 1603)

Under Section C – Annex 1603 of the USMCA, "Each Party shall grant temporary entry and provide confirming documentation to a business person employed by an enterprise who seeks to render services to that enterprise or a subsidiary or affiliate thereof, in a capacity that is managerial, executive or involves specialized knowledge, provided that the business person otherwise complies with the Party's measures applicable to temporary entry. A Party may require the business person to have been employed continuously by the enterprise for one year within the three-year period immediately preceding the date of the application for admission." These conditions are pretty much the same as NAFTA, namely:

- The company needs to do business both in the US or Mexico and in Canada

- The intra-company transferee must be in a managerial or executive position, or they need to show specialized knowledge within the company

- The intra-company transferee must show at least one year of full-time experience with the company in the past three years

Under the current NAFTA (exemption code T24), the intra-company transferee who is the US or Mexican citizen may receive a work permit that is valid for three years.

PROFESSIONALS (SECTION D – ANNEX 1603)

Appendix 1603.D.1 of the USMCA offers a list of professionals and their education requirements. Professionals may also work in Canada without an LMIA. However, they need a work permit. The duration of such work permit is usually 12 months or less.

TIP # 57: WORK PERMIT FOR TELEVISION AND FILM PRODUCTION WORKERS

Oliver is a professional sound engineer who works for a local TV station in Liverpool, UK. Oliver, a British citizen, is highly skilled and educated in the field of sound engineering. He is an active member of the Association of Motion Picture Sound (AMPS) in the United Kingdom. A TV station in Fredericton, New Brunswick has recently offered him a position in their company. He will be part of the production of a TV series for the Canadian Broadcasting Corporation (CBC). The Canadian TV station hopes to get a work permit for Oliver without going through the LMIA process.

The government of Canada decided to ease up the process of work permit for employees of TV and film production industry in 2016. If applicable to a person, they may apply for a work permit without an LMIA [note to practitioners: the exemption code is C14 under R205(a)].

If you intend to apply under this program, you need to consider the following points:

- This exemption code is for the television and film industry only
- The position or project needs to create significant benefits to

citizens or permanent residents of Canada

- These kinds of jobs are usually unionized in Canada. A letter from the relevant Union needs to support the hiring of the foreign national

- The employer needs to submit a detailed reference letter in support of the position and the foreign national

- The position must be a high-wage job. In other words, the salary of the foreign national must be equal or higher than the median salary of the Canadian province for the same position

The preceding list is neither exclusive nor conclusive. If you are not eligible to apply under this code, you could potentially apply under any of the following options:

- Work Permit for Performing Artists – Reciprocity Code C23 (see Tip # 59)

- Work without a work permit for performing artists under subsection 186(g) of IRPR (see Tip # 48)

- Work Permit under Significant Benefits to Canada – Code C10 (see Tip # 58)

- Applying for LMIA under high-wage positions (see Tip # 49)

TIP # 58: WORK PERMIT FOR SUCCESSFUL PEOPLE

Gazala is a famous Algerian author, political analyst, and speaker. She holds a Ph.D. in politics from University of Ouargla (Université Kasdi Merbah de Ouargla). She has written five books in French, two books in English, and three books in Arabic. She has delivered hundreds of speeches in Africa, Europe, Asia, and South America. Gazala is famous for her well-informed, pragmatic, and engaging speeches. She has attended interviews with hundreds of news outlets in the past few years. A Canadian news agency intends to hire Gazala as their African and Middle East senior director. She will work in their office in Halifax, Nova Scotia. The news agency wonders if they can skip the LMIA process and receive Gazala's work permit quickly.

When you intend to work in Canada, you usually need to go through a process called LMIA or rather getting a seal of approval from an ESDC officer (see Tip # 49). The LMIA process is time-consuming, costly, and prone to failure. Luckily, the government of Canada offers many LMIA exemption opportunities under the International Mobility Program or IMP (see Tip # 50).

The IMP programs come with several LMIA exemption codes. One of these codes is C10 or Canadian interests – Significant benefit.

JOBS FALLING UNDER SIGNIFICANT BENEFIT

The jobs that fall under this code needs to meet the following criteria.

- There are no other LMIA exemption codes for the position
- The job results in significant benefit to the social or cultural fabric of Canada
- The employer is not a frivolous employer

EMPLOYEES FALLING UNDER SIGNIFICANT BENEFIT

The employee needs to be extremely successful in their field. Their track record needs to show they can significantly contribute to the Canadian social, economic, or cultural fabric.

The officers heavily rely on external resources to approve the employee. For example, they look into referral letters from experts in the field and articles published on credible media outlets. They also look into the history and credentials of the applicant. They may also consider the applicant's educational background and their employment or business experience.

The officers tend to refuse requests and ask for an LMIA unless they find the answers to the following questions convincing:

- Has the applicant received any national or international awards or recognition?
- Do the current and previous employees attest to the relevance of the applicant's experience and skills to the offered position in Canada?
- Has the applicant ever been a judge of the works of others in their field?
- Has the applicant published research papers, books, or articles related to the offered position?
- Are the applicant's educational background and credentials significant and related to their area of expertise?

- Is the applicant a member of well-known national or international organizations in their field?
- Has the applicant ever led any organizations related to the offered position?

The preceding list is neither inclusive nor exclusive, but it can help you have an idea about a potentially successful candidate. Some candidates may not fall under this option, but they may qualify for other LMIA exemption codes. See Tip # 50 for more information about working in Canada without an LMIA.

TIP # 59: A SPECIAL WORK PERMIT FOR PERFORMING ARTISTS – RECIPROCITY

Oliver is a professional dancer. He is a British citizen who currently works for a Welsh dance company. Oliver recently received a job offer from a well-known opera company in Vancouver. They intend to hire him for one year. Oliver has seen Canadian performers on the UK stages before. He wonders if he could move to Canada and work there as a dancer for the Vancouver-based company.

Performing arts is an integral element of culture. Canada takes performing arts seriously. Here is a list of some variations of performing arts:

- **Theatrical performances** in the form of "plays, musicals, opera, ballet, illusion, mime, classical Indian dance, kabuki, mummers' plays, improvisational theatre, stand-up comedy, pantomime, and non-conventional or contemporary forms like postmodern theatre, post-dramatic theatre, or performance art[21]."
- **Dance** such as Latin or rhythm (e.g. Rumba, Salsa), swing dance (e.g. Balboa, Blues, Jive), Kumega Dance or traditional African and African-American dance (e.g. Traditional Jazz, Afro-beat, Boogie-woogie), ballroom dance (e.g. Tango, Waltz, Quickstep), classical Indian dance (e.g. Garba, Bharatanatyam, Yakshagana),

traditional Iranian Dance (e.g. Persian dance, Turkish dance), Azerbaijani dances (e.g. Anzali, Gaval, Youz bir), experimental or freestyle dances (e.g. Jump up), street dance (e.g. Floating, Flexing), disco or electronic dance (e.g. Hustle, Vogue), Pogo dance (e.g. Hard Rock Pogo), historical dance (e.g. Masque, Vintage dance), ethnic dance, folk dance, and so on (e.g. Hip Hop)[22].

- **Music** such as classical, pop, progressive, religious, rock, soul, jazz, blues, etc.

WORK PERMIT FOR PERFORMING ARTISTS

If a Canadian company that is active in performing arts hires a professional performing artist from abroad under the following conditions, the foreign national could receive a work permit to Canada without the need for an LMIA.

- "The employer is a current recipient of the core or composite funding from the Canada Council for the Arts or of financial support via parliamentary appropriation, such as the National Arts Centre."[23]
- The job offer is only for performing arts (note to practitioners; focus on NOC codes 5131, 5132, 5133, 5134, 5135, and 5232), preferably in the "dance, opera, orchestra or live theatre discipline of the arts."[24]
- The employee is a professional performing artist or a key element of the production (e.g. the director, the playwright, the librettist, the choreographer, or the set designer)
- There is enough evidence to prove reciprocity

RECIPROCITY IS THE KEY

Immigration authorities will issue the Work Permit without an LMIA only if they believe there are similar opportunities available to Canadian performers. For example, if the foreign performer is a German citizen in the field of opera, the immigration authorities want to see if similar opportunities exist for Canadian opera singers and performers in Germany.

It is the employer's responsibility to offer evidence to the immigration authorities in this regard. Sometimes you may refer to certain organizations for support letters. IRCC suggests the following[25]:

- **Dance**: Canadian Dance Assembly, International Alliance of Theatrical Stage Employees (IATSE), Canadian Actors' Equity Association, Regroupement québécois de la danse
- **Orchestral music**: Orchestras Canada, Canadian Federation of Musicians
- **Theatre**: IATSE, Canadian Actors' Equity Association, The Professional Association of Canadian Theatres
- **Opera**: Opera.ca, Canadian Actors' Equity Association

This list is neither inclusive nor exclusive. You may refer to other trustworthy resources for support letters or statistics. If the job offer meets all requirements, it will be exempt from an LMIA under the exemption code C23 (note to practitioners see R205(b)).

THE PROCESS

To receive a work permit under this program, you need to go through these steps:

1. The employer needs to create an account on the IRCC Employer Portal
2. The employer needs to register the job offer on the Employer Portal and pay the compliance fee of CAD 230 (fees subject to change)
3. The employer needs to prepare the work permit package for the employee
4. Depending on the nationality of the employee, they may apply at a port of entry, or they need to submit their application before or after entering Canada. Consult with a professional for more information. Most performing artists need to give biometrics as well. The current processing fee for a work permit is $155 and an additional $85 for the biometrics (some exceptions exist, fees subject to change)

OTHER OPTIONS

This method of work permit highly depends on the nature of the job, the credentials of the employer, and the existence of reciprocity. If you do not fall under this program, one of the following could be your option:

- Immigrating to Canada as a self-employed artist (see Tip # 32)

- Working in Canada without a work permit as part of a group of performing artists who are present in Canada for a short period (see Tip # 48)

- Getting a work permit without an LMIA under other exemption codes such as C16 or C11 (see Tips # 57 and 35 respectively)

- Getting a work permit supported by an LMIA (see Tip # 49)

---

[21] https://en.wikipedia.org/wiki/Performing_arts#Theatre
[22] https://en.wikipedia.org/wiki/List_of_dance_style_categories
[23] https://www.canada.ca/en/immigration-refugees-citizenship/corporate/publications-manuals/operational-bulletins-manuals/temporary-residents/foreign-workers/exemption-codes/canadian-interests-reciprocal-employment-performing-arts-r205-b-exemption-code-c23.html
[24] Same source as 23
[25] Same source as 23

TIP # 60: BUSINESS VISITORS TO CANADA

A Colombian company hires Jose in Medellin, Colombia. They use certain equipment they have purchased from a Canadian company in their production line. Jose is not quite familiar with the equipment. The Colombian company deploys Jose to Canada for two weeks. He learns about the tools they use at the Canadian location. The training is hands-on. Jose will be present at the production line, and he may even manufacture some products while going through the training. His Colombian employer will cover his travel expenses. While he is in Canada, he will receive his salary from his Colombian employer. Jose will then go back to Medellin and continue working for the Colombian company upon completion of the training. Does Jose need a work permit for his trip to Canada?

Canada, one of the powerhouses in technology and science, hosts thousands of successful businesses. Many of these businesses export their products and services to other regions in the world. The employees of their foreign customers may need to understand how to use the tools and goods they purchase from their Canadian suppliers. Consequently, they may visit Canada to receive training from their Canadian service providers. These people are among a large group of people who visit our country as business visitors.

WHO IS A BUSINESS VISITOR?

Millions of people visit Canada every year. Some of those people are business visitors, but who is a business visitor?

The main group of business visitors are probably those who enter Canada for international business without directly entering the Canadian labour market (subsection 187(1) of IRPR). An example is the CEO of a French company who visits Canada to meet with Canadian companies. She intends to meet with the decision-makers of those companies and discuss potential business opportunities such as selling the French company products or services to them or purchasing the Canadian companies' products or services. While she is visiting Canada, the Canadian companies won't cover her salary. They may, however, pay for her travel expenses.

Subsection 187(2) of the Immigration and Refugee Protection Regulations (IPRR) divides business visitors into three major groups:

- Group A – Purchasing or Training Activities
- Group B – Training at the Canadian Branch
- Group C – Business to Business (B2B) Sales

GROUP A – PURCHASING OR TRAINING ACTIVITIES

This group includes "foreign nationals purchasing Canadian goods or services for a foreign business or government or receiving training or familiarization in respect of such goods or services" (paragraph R187(1)(a)). It is important to make sure the training is for learning how to use Canadian products or services. I persist on this issue, because if a person attends an extended training program, they may need to receive a Study Permit. However, short-term training that are under six months and is not part of a certificate, diploma, or degree program does not call for a Study Permit.

Let's say a Canadian company manufactures a popular CNC machine. A Japanese company deploys three of its employees to Canada. They stay in Canada for two months. They receive special training on the CNC machine for six consecutive weeks. They eventually decide to purchase one of the machines. When they sign the deal, they return to Japan. The host company offers them accommodation, transportation, and meals while they are in Canada, but the Japanese company covers their salaries. This group of three are business visitors.

GROUP B – TRAINING AT THE CANADIAN BRANCH

If a Canadian company holds branches in other parts of the world, they may invite their foreign employees to the parent company from time to time. If the purpose of such visits is to either receive or give training, then the visitors are business visitors. Paragraph 187(1)(b) of IRPR describes this group as "foreign nationals receiving or giving training within a Canadian parent or subsidiary of the corporation that employs them outside Canada if any production of goods or services that results from the training is incidental."

As an example, a hypothetical Canadian company produces women's garments in Winnipeg and Johannesburg. They have recently started a new production line in Winnipeg. A similar production line will be installed in Johannesburg next year. The company invites fifty of their Johannesburg employees to Canada for one month. While in Canada, they learn hands-on experience on how to operate the new line. Although they are in Canada, they receive their salaries from the Johannesburg branch. This group are business visitors.

GROUP C – B2B SALES

Some people sell goods or services to other companies or governments. We call this activity B2B sales or rather Business to Business sales. A foreign national who visits Canada for B2B sales could be a business visitor.

According to paragraph 187(2)(c) of IRPR, a business visitor could be "foreign nationals representing a foreign business or government for the purpose of selling goods for that business or government if the foreign national is not engaged in making sales to the general public in Canada."

Adam represents an Italian company that produces new technology useful for firefighters. Adam visits Canada for four months. While he is in Canada, he visits many cities in Ontario and Nova Scotia. He meets with fire departments of those cities and tries to convince them to purchase the technology. He succeeds to some extent. His Italian employer covers all his expenses and salary while he is in Canada. Adam is a business visitor.

BUSINESS VISITORS AND INTERNATIONAL TREATIES

Canada has signed many international treaties such as USMCA (formerly

NAFTA), CETA, GATS, and bilateral FTAs. The definition of business visitors in those agreements could be different from section 187 of IRPR. For example, read Tip # 56 about the USMCA.

VISA REQUIREMENTS FOR BUSINESS VISITORS

Business visitors are exempt from obtaining a work permit. If the business visitor is a US citizen, they may enter Canada without a TRV or eTA. They, however, need to hold documents that show they fall under the definition of a business visitor. For most business visitors, holding an invitation letter from one or more Canadian corporations is a must.

If the business visitor is not a US citizen, they most likely need an eTA or a TRV, depending on their nationality or their country of residence. Sometimes the business visitor is inadmissible to Canada. In such situations, they could still visit Canada by applying for rehabilitation or TRP (see Tip # 79).

See also Tip # 61 for information on invitation letters for business visitors.

TIP # 61: INVITATION LETTER FOR BUSINESS VISITORS

Vihaan, an Indian citizen, is a senior project manager at Tanza Consultancy Group (TCG) in Mumbai[26]. The TCG branch in Toronto intends to run a two-day crash course on project management for some of their local employees. The training coordinator of the program believes Vihaan is the best fit for delivering the training. Vihaan does not hold a visa to visit Canada. He knows that as a business visitor, he is exempt from a work permit, but he still needs to apply for a TRV. He wonders how he can prove his intentions to the immigration officers.

An invitation letter is a great tool to show why someone is visiting Canada, who they are visiting, and how they are going to cover their expenses. Whether you are visiting Canada for personal reasons or as a business visitor, it is reasonable to obtain one or more invitation letters from an entity in Canada. As a reminder, one of the pillars of issuing a TRV is the purpose of the visit (see Tip # 14). A letter of invitation could clarify the purpose of the visit.

When it comes to business visitors, the issuance of the invitation letter is a must. The Canadian company that invites the business visitor must issue a formal invitation letter. I strongly recommend the following specifications for a business invitation letter.

- Make sure to use the Canadian company's letterhead for the invitation letter.
- The person who signs off the letter is the person who has the authority to invite the business visitor. In a small company this person is normally the director of the company, but in large companies, they could be the heads of one of the departments that have the authority to deal with other countries. Regardless of who signs the letter, it is not a bad idea if a second manager of the business ratifies the signature.
- The invitee must hold a copy of the letter for the port of entry. If they also need to apply for a TRV, the Canadian company may need to issue two copies of the invitation letter; one for the TRV application and one for presenting at the port of entry. If the TRV application is online, then one copy is enough as the invitee may carry the original to Canada.

There are three major elements in a typical business invitation letter, namely the *Canadian Company*, *the host*, and *the invitee*.

THE CANADIAN COMPANY

IRCC recommends the following to appear in the invitation letter about the Canadian company.

- Use of the company's letterhead which includes the name of the company
- The address of the headquarters of the company in Canada
- The addresses of all the branches of the company in Canada where the foreign national intends to visit
- A short description of the company's activities (make sure to enter the number of employees and other relevant information such as the year of the establishment of the company in Canada)
- Company's website address

THE HOST

You need to include the following about the host or rather the person who extends the invitation.

- Their name
- Their position in the company and their job title
- Contact information, including the phone number, business email address, and physical address of their place of work

THE INVITEE

- Their name, date of birth (if known)
- Their current employer and their position with that employer
- Their contact information (both work and home), including the phone number, email address, and physical address
- The relationship between the Canadian company and the invitee and if the host knows the invitee personally
- Why they are visiting Canada, their duration of visit, and the dates of entering and leaving Canada
- Who will take care of accommodation, transportation, and meals of the invitee?

An invitation letter does not guarantee the issuance of the visa, but it is extremely crucial for business visitors. Even if the visitor is visa exempt, they need to present an invitation letter to the Border Services Officers at the port of entry.

Also, see Tip # 60 for the definition of business visitors.

---

[26] A fictitious scenario. Any resemblance is incidental.

TIP # 62: OPEN WORK PERMIT

Akiki is a Ugandan citizen. Akiki's wife received a study permit to Canada four months ago and moved to Fredericton, New Brunswick. He misses his wife a lot and wants to join her in Canada. However, Akiki wonders if he could work in Canada while he is with his wife. He has heard an open work permit allows him to work for any employer, but he is not quite sure if he qualifies for an open work permit.

While some foreign nationals may work without a permit in Canada, the majority of them need a work permit. Working without a permit could result in a removal order from Canada. A typical work permit is limited to a specific employer, but an open work permit allows you to work for any employer.

WHAT IS AN OPEN WORK PERMIT?

Simply put, an open work permit allows a foreign national to work for any employer in Canada. However, an officer may impose some restrictions on an open work permit. For example, they may limit you to a specific geographical area. They might say you could only work in a specific city or a specific province. As another example, if you are suffering from certain medical conditions, the officer may prevent you from taking some jobs.

Regardless of the type of work permit, foreign nationals may not work in most adult industry jobs. Some examples include erotic massages, erotic or exotic dances, and escort services.

If you want to work with children or in healthcare professions, then you need to go through medical examination before applying for a work permit.

OPEN WORK PERMIT AND LMIA

All open-work-permit options are under the International Mobility Program (IMP). This program exempts applicants from an LMIA (see Tip # 50).

WHO MAY APPLY FOR AN OPEN WORK PERMIT?

The following people could apply for an open work permit.

- Applicants for permanent residency inside Canada. Some examples include Caregivers and in Canada class spousal or common-law sponsorship applicants
- People who are eligible for bridging work permits, such as certain Express Entry applicants
- Destitute students, or rather international students who have encountered unforeseen serious financial issues and need to work for a temporary duration
- A person who holds a TRP and the TRP is valid for at least six months (see Tip # 79)
- Refugee claimants, if they are under an unenforceable removal order
- Spouses or common-law partners of international students or foreign workers
- Students who are eligible for a Post Graduate Work Permit (see Tip # 72)
- Secondary and post-secondary co-op applicants
- Some workers that are eligible to apply because of reciprocal agreements with other countries, such as

- Working Holiday participants (International Experience Canada)
- Participants in Canada World Youth Program
- Some international athletes
- Family members of certain workers

- People who have applied for permanent residency under the Humanitarian and Compassionate (H&C) in Canada and the Minister has approved them under stage 1 of the process (see Tip # 47)
- Protected people, or rather those that IRB has approved their refugee claim and have applied for permanent residency

Of course, the list is very broad. The devil is in the details. Make sure to consult with a professional, before submitting your application.

WHERE TO APPLY FOR AN OPEN WORK PERMIT

If the applicant lives in Canada, they most likely may apply for the work permit from inside Canada. However, some exceptions could apply. If you are outside Canada, but you are from a visa-exempt country, you could apply at a port of entry. For the rest of the applicants, they have to apply before entering Canada.

THE APPLICATION PROCESS

The process of applying for an open work permit is similar to a regular work permit. There are some exceptions.

You need to clearly explain to the officer why you are eligible for an open work permit. I mention the exemption code and the sections of the Immigration and Refugee Protection Regulations that apply to the case.

You need to pay an extra $100 processing fee for the open work permit. Right now, the processing fee for a regular work permit is $155 and for an open-work-permit is $255. Most people need to pay $85 processing fee for the biometrics on top of the $255 processing fee. Just a quick reminder, the fees are always subject to change. Consult with the IRCC website for the official processing fees.

PART FOUR:
STUDYING IN CANADA

TIP # 63: STUDY PERMIT FOR INTERNATIONAL STUDENTS

Abigay, a Jamaican citizen, will complete her master's degree program at a respectable German university shortly. Abigay intends to continue her studies in Canada. She has already approached a University in Nova Scotia for a Ph.D. program that is close to her area of interest. Abigay knows she needs a study permit to study in Canada, but she has no clue what a study permit is and how she can receive it.

If you intend to study in Canada, you probably need a study permit. The following tip explains what a study permit is, who needs to apply for one, and who is exempt from it.

WHO NEEDS A STUDY PERMIT?

A foreign national who intends to study in Canada needs a study permit if the duration of the training program they are taking is more than six months. If the program finishes in less than six months, there is usually no need to apply for a study permit. Some examples of programs that call for a study permit are the following (assuming the duration is more than six months):

- A bachelor's, master's, or Ph.D. program at a university
- A post-secondary certificate or diploma at a private or community college
- Studying at an elementary or secondary school (at a private, boarding, or public school)

WHICH PROGRAMS ARE EXEMPT FROM A STUDY PERMIT?

If the program finishes under six months, you may not need a study permit. However, you may still need an eTA, a TRV, or a TRP to enter Canada. Some examples of such programs are the following:

- A one-week crash course about a specific subject
- A training seminar that lasts only a few days or a couple of weeks
- Attending an English as a Second Language (ESL) course or a French training course, if the program is less than six months and is not part of a 6+ months diploma program
- Taking a course that is a prerequisite to get admission to a post-secondary diploma or a university degree program. Please note that this specific course cannot be part of the diploma or degree and it is just the prerequisite.

WHAT IS THE DIFFERENCE BETWEEN A STUDY PERMIT AND A VISA?

Study permit allows the holder to stay in Canada and study. Visa is to enter Canada. If you are coming from a visa exempt country, then you may only need an eTA to enter Canada (US citizens do not even need an eTA). In this situation, you can apply for the study permit and if the permit is approved the immigration authorities will also issue you an eTA.

If you are from a country that you need a visa to enter Canada, you apply for a study permit and if you get approved the immigration authorities will issue you a TRV (see Tip # 14).

In both situations, when you reach a Canadian port of entry, you will receive a paper copy of the study permit. Remember that the study permit is not for re-entry. You may only enter Canada if you hold a valid eTA or TRV or TRP. As I mentioned earlier, US citizens are exempt from eTA or TRV, but some of them might need a TRP because of inadmissibility to Canada(see Tip # 79).

FOR HOW LONG IS A STUDY PERMIT VALID?

An immigration officer usually issues the study permit for the duration of your studies. However, you need to continue your studies actively, or you will lose it. If your study permit is expiring soon and you have not completed your studies yet, you could apply for a new study permit.

WHO MAY STUDY WITHOUT A PERMIT?

The following people may study in Canada without a permit.

- They are attending a program that is less than six months, and it is not part of a longer program
- Certain employees of foreign governments and their accompanying family members
- Minor children of parents who are in Canada with a valid work permit or study permit or if their parents are permanent resident or citizens of Canada
- Certain members of foreign armed forces who are working in Canada
- Permanent residents and citizens of Canada
- First Nations, Innuits, and Métis

If the duration of the course or program is less than six months, you may still apply for a study permit. The study permit allows you to work part-time while you are staying in Canada. However, for short programs, you need to justify the officer as to why you are requesting a study permit.

WHERE TO APPLY FOR A STUDY PERMIT

Everyone may apply for a study permit before entering Canada.

If you are a US citizen, a US permanent resident, a resident of Greenland, or a resident of St. Pierre and Miquelon, you may apply for study permit when entering Canada (see Tip # 65).

The following groups of people may apply for a study permit after entering Canada.

- They already hold a study or work permit
- They hold a TRP (a Temporary Resident Permit) that is valid for at least six months
- They are subject to an unenforceable removal order
- They are minors who would like to study at preschool, primary, or secondary school
- They are exchange students
- They have completed a prerequisite course in Canada and now wish to enroll in a program that is longer than six months
- They reside in Canada and have applied for permanent residency as a spouse or common-law partner in Canada class
- The immigration authorities have approved their refugee claim, and they have applied for permanent residency
- They have applied for permanent residency under Humanitarian and Compassionate (H&C) considerations, and they have received an initial approval
- They are family members of the last three groups mentioned above

IS EVERY LEARNING INSTITUTION ACCEPTABLE?

If you are studying at the preschool, elementary, or secondary level, you may select any school of your choice. If you are studying at the post-secondary level, you need to get admission from a Designated Learning Institution (see Tip # 64).

TIP # 64: DESIGNATED LEARNING INSTITUTIONS

Hala is a Jordanian high school student. She intends to continue her studies in Canada. Hala has researched several universities and colleges in Canada. But even so, she is not quite sure if she can trust any of those schools. Many of those schools ask for $100 or more to review her application for admission to the school. Hala has heard, she must look for a designated learning institution. She, however, does not know how to make sure the schools she finds are among them.

An international student is someone who is not a Canadian citizen or permanent resident but intends to study in Canada. Generally speaking, if the length of the study is less than six months and it is not part of a more extended program, you do not need a study permit. In these situations, you register to the program and enter Canada as a visitor. Of course, depending on your nationality, you may need a TRV or an eTA (see Tip #63).

If the length of study is more than six months, then a study permit becomes mandatory. If you are not familiar with the concept of study permit, see Tip # 63.

The first step in most study permit applications is to receive admission from a Designated Learning Institution (DLI). But what is a DLI and how can you locate them?

WHAT IS A DESIGNATED LEARNING INSTITUTION (DLI)?

IRCC approves certain education providers as DLIs. A Provincial body usually gives accreditation to these institutions. A typical DLI also has a few years of experience in the field of education. Each Designated Learning Institution has a DLI number. Here are some examples of actual DLI numbers:

- Burman University in Lacombe, Alberta – O19390898172
- Ashton College in Vancouver, British Columbia – O19219876582
- Canadian Mennonite University in Winnipeg, Manitoba – O19021102272
- Yukon College in Ross River, Yukon – O19604209351
- Holland College in Charlottetown, Prince Edward Island – O19220082122

Of course, these are only a few samples.

As you can see, each DLI number begins with the letter "O" followed by 11 digits. Sometimes a college or university has more than one campus. For example, the University of Toronto has three locations. One of them is in downtown Toronto, the other one is in Scarborough, and the last one is in Mississauga. All of them have the same DLI number though, O19332746152.

When you look up a college or university make sure your target campus has a valid DLI number.

HOW TO LOCATE A DLI?

The IRCC website has a page that locates all DLIs. To find that page, visit the following link:

settler.ca/88/dli

WHAT ABOUT PRIMARY AND SECONDARY SCHOOLS?

All primary and secondary schools in Canada are designated learning institutions. They do not have a DLI number, and you do not need to present a DLI for them when you apply for a study permit. Make sure the school you are registering is a respectable and reliable institution.

WHAT IS PGWP-ELIGIBLE?

If you look at the DLI table on the IRCC website, the last column says "Offers PGWP-eligible Programs." PGWP stands for Post-Graduate Work Permit. Suppose you finish your studies in Canada. If the program you have taken is eligible for PGWP, you could apply for an open work permit (conditions apply).

If you receive a PGWP, you may stay in Canada and work for any employer. A PGWP could potentially open doors for your permanent residency under some provincial programs or the Express Entry (especially the Canadian Experience Class subcategory). See Tip # 72 for more information.

:

TIP # 65: APPLYING FOR STUDY PERMIT AT A PORT OF ENTRY

Janet is a US citizen. She recently got admission to a Master of Laws program in Canada. She already has paid her first-year tuition fee. Janet has enough financial resources to cover her expenses in Canada. She even has leased an apartment in downtown Toronto, close to her school. Janet knows she needs a study permit to study in Canada legally. She wonders if she can apply for the study permit while she enters Canada via the Niagara Rainbow land crossing.

Canada is a large country with hundreds of official border crossings also known as ports of entry (see Tip # 10). Canadian ports of entry (POE) include international airports, rail crossings, land crossings, ferry crossings, and sea or lake ports. Most of these ports are between Canada and the United States.

If you want to study in Canada and the duration of your studies is more than six months you need to apply for a study permit (see Tip # 63). You usually need to receive an admission from a designated learning institution in Canada and also prove to the immigration authorities you meet the financial requirements and do not intend to stay in Canada illegally.

When you have all your documents ready you may apply at a POE only if you are,

- A US citizen,

- A Permanent Resident of the United States or rather a Green Card holder,

- A person who has been lawfully admitted to the United States for permanent residence,

- A resident of St. Pierre and Miquelon, or

- A resident of Green Land. (practitioners see R214)

Other people may not apply for Study Permit at a POE. Alternative options for them is applying before entering Canada and in some exceptional situations after entering Canada.

If you are eligible to apply at a POE you need to have all the necessary documents with you at the time of crossing the border, namely:

- **Proof of Acceptance**: Admission letter from a Designated Learning Institution (DLI) in Canada (see Tip # 64)

- **Proof of Financial Support for at least One Year**: Documents that show you can pay your tuition fee, living expenses, and other expenses such as your textbooks, etc. Although you may work in Canada, you need to show you can take care of yourself without working. For example, you can show your bank statements, scholarship or bursary documents, financial documents of the person who supports you (such as their salary payslips, or bank statements), the receipt of the payment of the first semester tuition fee or the residence fee (if applicable), or any other documents that convinces the officer you won't face financial problems in Canada.

- **Proof of Identity**: You need to present a valid passport. It is also a good idea to have a secondary government-issued document or ID such as a driver's licence

- **Letter of explanation**: On a letter, explain why you intend to study in Canada and show you are aware of your responsibilities as an international student (e.g. engaging in full-time studies, not committing any illegal activities, no interruptions in your studies, and leaving Canada upon completion of your studies)

- **Custodian declaration for minor children**: Minor children who study in Canada need to have a Custodian.

- **Certificat d'acceptation du Québec (CAQ)**: If you intend to study in the province of Quebec you need to obtain a CAQ from the Province and present it to the Border Services Officer.

- **Other Documents**: Bring other supporting documents with you, such as:
    - Two passport size photos (as a backup)
    - Use of a Representative form duly signed by you and your representative (e.g. an RCIC), if you have one. If you encounter any problems at the border the form proves you have a representative and potentially encourages the border services officer to call your representative to resolve the issues.
    - Marriage certificate (if you are married): If your spouse accompanies you, then this document is extremely important because he or she could receive a visitor record or even an open work permit while you are studying in Canada.
    - For common-law partners, documents that prove your relationship. For example, a signed Statutory Declaration of Common-law Union form, bills that show both names with the same address, the government issued cards or documents that show similar addresses for both, joint rental or lease agreements, or joint ownership of properties or vehicles
    - Job offers from your existing employer that shows you have the intention to go back to your home country upon completion of your studies (not mandatory but helpful)
    - Police clearance report from your home country and every country you have lived in for more than six months since the age of 18 (not mandatory but helpful)
    - Documents that show you can complete your studies in Canada (e.g. English language test results, GMAT test results, high school diploma, etc.)

NOTE: This is not an official document checklist. You need to consult with your immigration consultant or the IRCC website before entering Canada.

FEES

Remember you need to pay the processing fee at the POE. They usually accept major credit cards, but I highly advise having cash with you as well. You will likely pay the following:

- 150 CAD processing for the study permit
- 255 CAD processing fee for your spouse/common-law open work permit (if applicable)
- 85 CAD biometrics fee (does not apply to US citizens) – See Tip # 12 for more details about biometrics

OPEN WORK PERMIT FOR THE SPOUSE

If your spouse or common-law partner apply for an open work permit, make sure they have the following documents with them. They may apply for an open work permit at the border only if they are exempt from a visa to enter Canada (e.g. they are US, UK, Japan, or Italy citizens)

- Marriage certificate or proof of common-law relationship (please see the previous bullet points for more information)
- Two passport size photos (as a backup)
- Identity documents (valid passport and one backup document such as a driver's licence)
- Police clearance report from their home country and every country they have lived in for more than six months since the age of 18 (not mandatory but helpful)
- Documents that show they have enough qualifications to work in Canada (e.g. educational credentials, work reference letters from the previous employer, etc.)

NOTE: This is not an official document checklist. You need to consult with your immigration consultant or the IRCC website before entering Canada.

CRIMINAL HISTORY

If you have any criminal history, you could be inadmissible to Canada. Consult with a professional before applying for a study permit. Sometimes your best option is to apply for rehabilitation or a Temporary Resident Permit before entering Canada. The US and Canada share information. You don't want awkward moments at the POE and worse than that removal from Canada.

MEDICAL HISTORY

If you have a history of medical issues (physical or mental), you need to consult with a professional. In some cases, it is better to go through a medical examination before entering Canada.

TIP # 66: APPLYING FOR STUDY PERMIT WITHIN CANADA

Bernita is an Ecuadorian citizen. She and her husband moved to Canada last summer because her husband received a work permit to work for a financial company in Windsor, Ontario. Bernita holds a bachelor's degree. She wants to continue her studies in Canada. She approached the University of Windsor and received admission from them. Bernita wonders if she could apply for study permit within Canada. She doesn't want to leave Canada as it imposes lots of expenses and forces her to be away from her husband for a while.

As a general rule, you need to apply for a study permit while you are outside Canada. However, there are some exceptional situations. For example, some people may apply for a study permit when they are entering Canada (see Tip # 65). The focus of this article is on those people who may apply for a study permit from within Canada.

You may apply for a study permit within Canada, if,

- you already hold a valid study permit or work permit;
- your study permit expired less than 90 days ago, but you are the minor child of a foreign worker or international student;
- your study permit expired less than 90 days ago, but you are the

family member of a foreign diplomat;

- you hold a temporary resident permit that is valid for at least six months;
- you are under an unenforceable removal order;
- IRB has conferred your refugee application, or rather you are a protected person;
- you hold a temporary resident status, and you meet one of the following conditions:
    o studying at preschool, primary school, or secondary school (practically only minor children)
    o a visiting student to a designated learning institution
    o completed a course of study in Canada that is a prerequisite for a more extended program
- your in-Canada class spousal sponsorship application is under review, but not finalized;
- you have successfully passed the stage one of an H&C application (see Tip # 47); or
- you are a family member of a protected person, an in-Canada class spousal sponsorship applicant, or a person whose H&C application has successfully passed the stage one.

WHAT IF YOU CANNOT APPLY WITHIN CANADA?

If none of the above applies, you may still submit your paper application to the Visa Application Centre in Los Angeles. Alternatively, you need to leave Canada and apply from outside Canada. The latter is probably a better option for most applicants.

TIP # 67: THE STUDY DIRECT STREAM (SDS) PROGRAM

Gabriel is a Filipino. He recently finished his bachelor's degree and wants to pursue his master's degree in Canada. Gabriel wonders if there are special measures that apply to him.

Canada launched a new program for study permits in 2018. This program could make the process faster and easier for certain applicants. The new Study Direct Stream (SDS) Program covers the legal residents of the following countries:

- China
- India
- the Philippines
- Vietnam

This program may expand to other countries in the future (Kenya and Senegal could be the next two countries). If you are not a legal resident of the approved countries, you may not apply for SDS, and you need to apply under the regular study permit processes. To qualify for this program, you also need to meet the following requirements.

- Take a medical exam through an approved Panel Physician
- Purchase a $10,000 GIC (Guaranteed Investment Certificate) from a Canadian Bank. Currently, Scotiabank, ICICI Bank Canada, and SBI Canada Bank are the only participating Canadian financial institutions in this program.
- Get admission to a Designated Learning Institution in Canada (see Tip # 64)
- Pay the first-year tuition fee in full
- Take the IELTS with a score of at least 6 or take the TEF with a score equivalent to Niveaux de compétence linguistique canadiens 7. If you have graduated from a Canadian curriculum high school, you are exempt from taking any of these tests.
- Submit other necessary forms and documents

The forms and document checklists vary depending on your country of residence. Consult with the IRCC website or a professional to help you with the process. Keep in mind, SDS does not guarantee success but is a faster method to receive a response to your application.

TIP # 68: COMMUNITY COLLEGES VERSUS PRIVATE COLLEGES

Sarifina is a citizen of Liberia. She has recently completed her high school diploma. Sarifina wants to pursue her studies at a Canadian college. She googled many colleges and realized some of them are community colleges and some of them are private. She doesn't quite know the difference.

Canada is famous for its high-quality educational system. Hundreds of thousands of international students study in Canadian institutions every year. Many of these students start their education at the post-secondary (tertiary) level. They complete their high school or secondary diploma in their home country, and then they continue their post-secondary training in Canada at a university or a college. Canadian colleges offer the following opportunities to international students.

- Post-secondary diplomas (also known as associate degrees)
- Post-secondary certificates
- Post-graduate diplomas or certificates (i.e. you need to complete a higher education program first and then attend these programs)

- Short-term training and crash courses
- Skills trades training (e.g. welding, plumbing, etc.)
- Prep courses for professional licences exams
- Bachelor's degree programs (under the supervision or with the collaboration of a university)
- English as a Second Language (ESL) training
- French language training

This list does not show all the options. Visit the colleges' websites for more potential options.

WHAT IS A COMMUNITY COLLEGE?

Canada consists of ten provinces and three territories, namely British Columbia, Alberta, Saskatchewan, Manitoba, Ontario, Quebec, New Brunswick, Nova Scotia, Prince Edward Island, Newfoundland and Labrador, Northwest Territories, Yukon, and Nunavut.

The Canadian provinces financially support some of the colleges in their province. These publicly-funded colleges are community colleges. They may receive funds from the federal government of Canada or other sources as well. Due to the funds they receive, the community colleges may reduce their tuition fees.

WHAT IS A PRIVATE COLLEGE?

Private colleges do not receive funds from the federal or provincial governments. They rely on tuition fees to run their business. Most provinces use rigorous procedures to accredit these colleges.

Private colleges are usually smaller than community colleges and more expensive for local students. Private colleges in the province of Ontario are called Private Career Colleges (PCC) as they focus on skills development for specific career opportunities.

PROS AND CONS OF STUDYING IN PRIVATE VERSUS COMMUNITY COLLEGES

The following list compares community and private colleges from different angles for international students.

- **Tuition Fee**: Community colleges are usually cheaper options comparing to private colleges. However, when it comes to international students, the tuition fee is not much different between them. In some cases, you may even find a private college that is cheaper than a community college.

- **Class sizes**: The number of students in private colleges is usually a lot less than community colleges. Of course, exceptions apply.

- **Length of education**: Many private colleges strive to offer similar programs to community colleges in shorter periods without compromising the quality of education. This approach saves you time and also could compensate for higher tuition fees to some extent. The shorter education time means you spend a lot less on food, accommodation, and transportation. You also achieve your educational goals faster.

- **Admission**: The only source of income for private colleges is their students. They are always thirsty for new students and consequently more flexible towards giving them admission.

- **Designation by the Immigration Authorities**: The immigration authorities recognize all community colleges. As an international student, you may only register to Designated Learning Institutions (DLI) to be able to secure a Study Permit. Some private colleges may not be DLIs. To make sure if the immigration authorities designate a college or not visit the IRCC website (see Tip # 64). For local students, the designation by IRCC is not important.

- **Working while studying in Canada**: If you hold a valid study permit, you may work up to 20 hours per week while studying in Canada. You may even work full-time during normal breaks such as winter and spring breaks. This opportunity is available to both community and private colleges.

- **Educational credential assessment (ECA)**: As an international student you might want to eventually immigrate to

Canada and become a Permanent Resident of Canada. Some methods of immigration (e.g. the Express Entry) expect you evaluate your educational credentials through an approved organization, also known as ECA. If you complete your education in Canada, you do not need to go through the ECA process. This feature is the same for both private and community colleges. However, the institution must hold a DLI number.

- **Post-graduate Work Permit**: If you are an international student and graduate from a community college you may apply for a special work permit (PGWP) to stay in Canada and work after graduation. This option is rarely available to private colleges. Visit the IRCC website to make sure your prospect college qualifies for a PGWP after completion of your studies (see Tip # 72).

TIP # 69: THE BEST UNIVERSITIES IN CANADA

Mateo is a citizen of Uruguay. He intends to complete an MBA program in Canada. Mateo insists on studying in the best Canadian university. He believes graduation from a great university will open lots of opportunities for him.

Canada is among the top destinations for international post-secondary students. We can probably consider the following reasons for this high rank.

- One of the top economies in the world
- Education in two major languages of English and French
- A diverse country that is open to all different cultural backgrounds
- The permission to work while you are studying
- The possibility of immigration to Canada when your studies are over

While many Canadian universities shine in the world of education, the following list shows those universities that are famous for their enthusiasm for research. These universities are all publicly funded. They are also famously known as U15 (the members of an association in Ottawa that encourages undertaking research activities).

Name of the University	City	Province	Website
University of Alberta	Edmonton	Alberta	ualberta.ca
University of British Columbia	Vancouver	British Columbia	ubc.ca
University of Calgary	Calgary	Alberta	ucalgary.ca
Dalhousie University	Halifax	Nova Scotia	dal.ca
Université Laval	Quebec City	Quebec	ulaval.ca
University of Manitoba	Winnipeg	Manitoba	umanitoba.ca
McGill University	Montreal	Quebec	mcgill.ca
McMaster University	Hamilton	Ontario	mcmaster.ca
Université de Montréal	Montreal	Quebec	umontreal.ca
University of Ottawa	Ottawa	Ontario	uottawa.ca
Queen's University	Kingston	Ontario	queensu.ca
University of Saskatchewan	Saskatoon	Saskatchewan	usask.ca
University of Toronto	Toronto	Ontario	utoronto.ca
University of Waterloo	Waterloo	Ontario	uwaterloo.ca
University of Western Ontario	London	Ontario	uwo.ca

If you want to study at any of these great universities, visit their websites and initiate your research about the programs they offer, their tuition fees, and their admission requirements.

Many other Canadian universities are great too. Not being on this list does not mean the institution is low-quality.

TIP # 70: STUDYING IN CANADA AS A MINOR (PRIMARY AND HIGH SCHOOL)

Chimango is a 12-year old Malawian boy. He is accompanying his parents to Canada. Chimango's father is in Canada on a work permit, and his mother is an international student. They currently live in Hamilton, Ontario close to McMaster University. Chimango's parents wonder if he may go to school and study in Canada. As a minor, he needs to receive a proper education.

Canada supports the best interest of children, but when it comes to children's education, not every child is entitled to study in Canada. This tip refers to children who are minor and would like to study at the pre-school, primary or secondary levels.

WHO IS A MINOR CHILD?

A child who has not reached the age of majority is a minor. Interestingly, the age of majority varies in different parts of Canada. Look at the following table for more information.

Age of Majority	Province or Territory of Canada
18	Alberta, Manitoba, Saskatchewan, Ontario, Quebec, Prince Edward Island
19	British Columbia, Yukon, Northwest Territories, Nunavut, New Brunswick, Nova Scotia, Newfoundland and Labrador

While the age of majority is 19 in some of the provinces and territories, it is safer if you consider 18 across the board.

WHICH GROUP OF CHILDREN MAY STUDY IN CANADA WITHOUT A STUDY PERMIT?

The following minor children may study at the pre-school, primary school, or secondary school (high school) without a study permit.

- Children who are citizens or permanent residents of Canada
- Children whose one of their parents is a citizen or permanent resident of Canada
- Refugees or refugee claimants accompanying their parents
- Accompanying children of refugees or refugee claimants
- Children who attend kindergarten (JK or SK)
- Minors who attend a training program that is less than six months (not a regular school program)
- Children without status
- Children whose one of their parents holds a valid study permit or work permit to Canada

If the child is not a Canadian citizen or permanent resident of Canada, they need a visitor record to stay and study in Canada.

Three groups of minor children need study permits to attend a school in Canada.

- Children who accompany parents who are both visitors in Canada
- Children who attend a school in Canada and none of their

- parents are accompanying them to Canada
- Children who attend post-secondary education, regardless of their age

HOW TO APPLY FOR A STUDY PERMIT?

If your child needs a study permit, then you normally need to apply for them from outside Canada. Although paragraph 215(1)(f)(i) of the Immigration and Refugee Protection Regulations allows a minor child to apply for a study permit within Canada, I have sometimes noticed immigration officers refuse these applications and advise the child to apply from outside Canada. Consult with a professional to make sure applying from inside Canada is an option.

IS AN ADMISSION FROM A SCHOOL NECESSARY?

If the child needs a study permit, then they need to get admission from a school first. Remember that all pre-schools, secondary schools, and primary schools in Canada are Designated Learning Institutions. Regardless, it is your responsibility as a parent to make sure you are enrolling your child to a respectable and reliable school.

HOW TO EXTEND THE STUDY PERMIT?

You need to apply for a new study permit before the expiry of the old one. The process for the new study permit is quite similar to the previous one. In other words, you need to get an admission for the child and apply for a study permit. However, you may apply from within Canada. If the child finishes secondary school and wants to study at a college or university, you need to apply for a new study permit regardless of the validity of the existing study permit.

DO I NEED TO PAY TUITION FEE?

If the child is exempt from a study permit, they are usually exempt from tuition fee as well. Nonetheless, double check with the local school board as their policy could be different.

Those children who need a study permit from Canada, have to pay the tuition fee. Also, bursary or scholarship is rarely available to minor children. You may give it a try, but it is less likely you get a scholarship or bursary.

DOES A MINOR CHILD NEED A CUSTODIAN?

If the parents or legal guardians of minor children do not accompany them to Canada, they need a custodian in Canada. Custodians are adult Canadian citizens or permanent residents who are trustworthy. They will be responsible for the well-being of the child. Of course, children also need a roof on their head and food to eat. If the parents or legal guardians do not accompany the children, they usually find homestay for them. Homestay means the child stays with a reliable Canadian family while they are in Canada.

CAN MINOR STUDENT WORK IN CANADA?

The short answer to this question is "no."

TIP # 71: WORKING WHILE STUDYING IN CANADA

Magdalena is an international student at Humber College in Toronto. She is a Finish citizen. Magdalena whose friends call her Leena is doing a two-year business program which will lead to a post-secondary diploma. She started her studies only a few weeks ago. Of course, like most other international students, Leena needs to work to cover part of her expenses. In spite of some research, she is not quite sure if she can work off-campus. Leen also doesn't know if she needs to apply for a work permit.

Canada is a huge magnet for international students. Relatively low tuition fees and living costs, the high quality of education, and the ability to work while you are studying are some enticing reasons to choose Canada for your studies. Of course, as an international student, you could eventually immigrate to Canada. Before you get too excited, make sure to read the rest of this tip.

WHICH STUDENTS MAY WORK IN CANADA?

As a rule of thumb, if you meet all the following requirements, you may work while you are studying in Canada.

- You are a full-time student;
- your study permit is valid;
- you are studying at a post-secondary level; and
- your school is a designated learning institution.

Also, if you have completed your studies, you may continue working in Canada, if you meet the following criteria,

- Your study permit is still valid; and
- You have applied for a post-graduate work permit (PGWP), but an officer has not rendered a decision on your PGWP application (see Tip # 72).

WHICH STUDENTS MAY NOT WORK IN CANADA?

Generally speaking, if you do not meet the requirements of the previous headline, you may not work in Canada, but to be clear, you may not work if any of the following applies to you.

- You are a minor;
- you are studying at pre-school, primary school, or secondary school levels;
- your school is not a designated learning institution;
- you are not a full-time student;
- your study permit is not valid;
- you have completed your studies and have not applied for a PGWP; or
- your education does not require a study permit, and you have not asked for one.

Remember, that even if only one of the above applies to you, working in Canada is not an option.

WHAT ARE THE CONDITIONS ON WORKING AS A STUDENT?

You may work on campus or off-campus. Also, you may work up to 20 hours per week during your studies and full-time during regular school breaks (e.g. the winter break). You usually can work for any employer in your region. However, IRCC prohibits you from working for businesses that are mainly in the adult industry. Some examples include exotic dances, escort services, and erotic massages. You may not even work as an accountant or a marketing manager for those businesses.

When you receive your study permit, make sure to read all the conditions posted on it. Sometimes the limitations are more than what I described above.

WHAT ABOUT INTERNSHIP OR CO-OP WORK?

Sometimes as part of your study, you need to work for an employer as an intern or a co-op student. Unfortunately, you need a work permit for those activities. Fortunately, you may apply from within Canada. You usually receive an open work permit for internship or co-op work.

WHAT IF MY CIRCUMSTANCES CHANGE?

Unwanted matters could happen in anybody's life. Suppose, you suddenly lose your financial support from your home country due to some severe and unforeseen situation. For example, an internal war erupts in your home country, or your family goes bankrupt. In these circumstances, you may apply for a work permit as a destitute student. Such work permits are open (see Tip # 62). They help you overcome your financial problems and go back to your studies as soon as you can.

TIP # 72: POST-GRADUATE WORK PERMIT

Armin is an international student in Canada. He is a citizen of Turkmenistan. Armin will soon finish his Bachelor of Science in Engineering program at the University of Saskatchewan. Although he dreams about getting his Ph.D., he prefers to become a Canadian as soon as possible. Someone told Armin, he may apply for a Post-Graduate Work Permit (PGWP) right after the school. He may then gain enough work experience to apply for permanent residency of Canada under the Canadian Experience Class (see Tip # 25). No doubt, Armin is excited to know more about the PGWP.

Canada competes with many other great economies of the world over the young talent. A significant source of this talent is international students. As a result, Canada has some measures in place to encourage these students to remain in Canada and become part of our social fabric. One of these measures is the Post-Graduate Work Permit.

WHAT IS A POST GRADUATE WORK PERMIT (PGWP)?

A PGWP is an open work permit that allows you to work in Canada for any employer. Of course, the immigration officer may impose some limitations on what you can do and the region you may work. The length of a PGWP depends on the length of your studies, and it is usually between one to three years.

WHO MAY APPLY FOR A PGWP?

You could apply for a PGWP if all of the following conditions apply:

- You completed a full-time post-secondary program in Canada;
- your program qualifies for a PGWP;
- you completed your studies in less than 90 days before applying for a PGWP;
- your school is a designated learning institution;
- you are at least 18 years old;
- you have never applied for PGWP in the past;
- the length of your program was at least eight months; and
- your study permit was valid when you applied for the PGWP.

If a program is normally eight months or more, but you take the accelerated version and finish it in less than eight months, you may still be eligible to apply for a PGWP.

WHO MAY NOT APPLY FOR A PGWP?

Of course, if you do not meet the requirements of the previous headline, you cannot apply for a PGWP. On top of that, you may not apply for a PGWP if any of the following is correct about you.

- Your studies were not continuous (for example, you took a year off and went back home);
- you received funding from or were part of any of the following:
  - The Government of Canada Awards Program funded by Global Affairs Canada (GAC);
  - the Canadian Commonwealth Scholarship Program funded by GAC;
  - the Canada-China Scholars Exchanges Program;

- - the Equal Opportunity Scholarship, Canada-Chile;
  - the Organization of American States Fellowships Program; or
  - any funding from GAC.
- most of your program was online or through distance learning; or
- you had applied for a PGWP in the past, following another study program.

As you can see, PGWP is a one-time opportunity, so use it wisely.

WHAT KINDS OF EDUCATIONAL PROGRAMS ARE ELIGIBLE FOR PGWP?

A typical educational program that is eligible for PGWP is full-time, continuous, more than eight months, and via a designated learning institution. Besides, the school usually needs to be one of the following:

- publicly funded post-secondary institutions such as universities, colleges, trade schools, or technical schools;
- certain private secondary or post-secondary schools in Quebec;
- private schools that may award bachelors, masters, or doctorate degrees approved by the province.

Instead of doing guesswork, look up the school from the IRCC website and see if they offer PGWP approved programs. Also, call the school to double check. The following link leads you to a page that allows you to look up schools for their DLI numbers and eligibility for PGWP:

settler.ca/88/dli

CAN I EXTEND MY PGWP?

Unfortunately, this is not an option. However, you could apply for another work permit from within Canada if you have a valid job offer supported by an LMIA, or if the job offer is exempt from LMIA. Of course, if you apply for immigration under Express Entry, you could qualify for a bridging work permit under certain circumstances.

PART FIVE:
IMMIGRATION ISSUES

TIP # 73: REMOVAL ORDERS – DEPORTATION, EXCLUSION, DEPARTURE

Anastasiya is a Bulgarian citizen. She entered Canada as an international student last year. Anastasiya was driving her car six months ago when a police officer stopped her. The officer tested Anastasiya's blood alcohol level and realized it was way above the permitted limit. She received a conviction later at a local court. Anastasiya will now face a removal hearing. She is worried about her future in Canada.

Sometimes the immigration authorities find you inadmissible to Canada (see Tip # 81). Keep in mind that inadmissibility affects foreign nationals and permanent residents only. Canadian citizens are in the safe zone. If you are inadmissible and you are already inside Canada, you may receive a removal order. A removal order is an official order that asks you to leave Canada within a limited period (usually within the next 30 days or less).

ENFORCEABLE VS. UNENFORCEABLE REMOVAL ORDERS

If a removal order is enforceable, you need to leave Canada as soon as possible. If the deadline on an enforceable removal order passes and you do not leave Canada, the CBSA will issue a nation-wide warrant for you. They will ask all police forces such as the RCMP, provincial police, or municipal police to arrest you and arrange your deportation from Canada.

Sometimes a removal order becomes unenforceable. An unenforceable removal order means you can stay in Canada until it becomes enforceable. If the authorities make a removal order void, you do not need to leave Canada (unless due to other reasons such as expiry of your permit). The following actions could make a removal order unenforceable.

- Judicial Review (practitioners see R231)
- Pre-removal Risk Assessment or PRRA (practitioners see R232)
- Humanitarian and compassionate or public policy considerations (practitioners see R233)

Some exceptions may apply. Consult with a professional for more information.

TYPES OF REMOVAL ORDERS

A removal order could be any of the following:

- **Departure Order**: You need to leave Canada within the next 30 days and report your departure to a Border Services Officer (or similar officials). If you do not leave Canada in the specified time or if you do not report your departure, the departure order turns into a deportation order automatically (practitioners see R224).
- **Exclusion Order**: You need to leave Canada within the specified time and do not get back to Canada within the next 12 months. In case of exclusion orders due to misrepresentation, you may not return to Canada within the next five years (practitioners see R225)
- **Deportation Order**: You need to leave Canada within the specified time, and you may not return to Canada unless you receive an Authorization to Return to Canada or an ARC (practitioners see R226)

AUTHORIZATION TO RETURN TO CANADA (ARC)

If you have received a departure order, you may return to Canada at any time subject to the following:

- You left Canada within the 30-day time limit
- You reported your departure
- You are not inadmissible to Canada
- You have proper permits or visas to return to Canada (e.g. you hold a valid eTA, TRV, Work Permit, Study Permit, or a Permanent Resident Visa). If you are a US citizen and you intend to visit Canada only, you do not need to hold a visa or eTA.

If you have received an exclusion order, but you left Canada a long time ago (i.e. at least 60 months ago for misrepresentation and 12 months ago for other situations), you may return to Canada subject to the conditions explained in the previous bullet points.

If you have received an exclusion order but the time limitation has not passed, or if you have received a deportation order, you need to apply for Authorization to Return to Canada (ARC) to return to Canada. A typical ARC application looks like a TRV application, but you need to pay the ARC processing fee (currently $400) and include several other documents to convince the immigration authorities you deserve the ARC.

For more information about an ARC application, see Tip # 74.

TIP # 74: AUTHORIZATION TO RETURN TO CANADA

Delmy is a citizen of El Salvador. She entered Canada on a visitor visa three years ago, but she didn't leave Canada in a timely fashion. Delmy could stay up to six months, but she stayed for more than two years. Then a car accident in downtown Calgary exposed her status to the police. Unfortunately, the CBSA officers detained Delmy under the immigration law and eventually issued her an exclusion order. She left Canada about six months ago. Delmy wants to go back to Canada as soon as she can. She is in a common-law relationship with a Canadian citizen. They also want to initiate a spousal sponsorship as soon as they can. Delmy has heard about the Authorization to Return to Canada application. She hopes this apply to her and she joins her common law very soon.

Life is full of twists and turns. Sometimes these anomalies put you in trouble. When it comes to immigration issues, governments are usually very harsh. Consequently, while you are in Canada, you need to do your best to avoid immigration problems, but if you don't, then you could receive a removal order from Canada.

Removal orders are the outcome of inadmissibility or non-compliance with the Immigration Act (IRPA). Generally, there are three types of removal orders: departure, exclusion, and deportation (see Tip # 73). An enforced removal order means you need to leave Canada as soon as possible. You also need to report your departure from Canada to a border officer upon leaving the country.

WHAT IS AN AUTHORIZATION TO RETURN TO CANADA?

When you receive a removal order, you usually need to receive an Authorization to Return to Canada (ARC) before being able to return to Canada. The following table shows if ARC is necessary for an enforced removal order.

Removal Order	ARC Necessary?
Departure	No
Exclusion	Yes, within the first 12 months
Exclusion (due to Misrepresentation)	Yes, within the first 60 months
Deportation	Yes, at any time

If you receive a departure order and you do not comply with the conditions, then it turns into a deportation order. Non-compliance with the departure order means you did not leave within 30 days of the enforcement of the departure order or you did not report your departure. If you want to know more about removal orders or inadmissibility to Canada, read the following Tips:

- Tip # 73: Removal Orders Canada
- Tip # 81: Who is Inadmissible to Canada?
- Tip # 80: Misrepresentation to Canada

The family members of the person who receives deportation or exclusion order could be exempt from the ARC. Consult with a professional for more information.

WHEN DOES THE COUNTDOWN BEGIN?

As you can see, there is a countdown for exclusion orders, or rather 12 months for a regular one and 60 months for a misrepresentation one. When you leave Canada, you need to meet with an officer. The officer issues a Certificate of Departure. Consequently, the start date for the countdown is the date on that certificate.

WHAT IS AN ARC APPLICATION?

An ARC application looks like a regular Temporary Resident Visa (TRV) application. However, the processing fee is $400 compared to $100 for a TRV. You also need to submit a letter and some documents to convince the immigration officer you deserve an ARC. Even if you are a US citizen or from a visa-exempt country, you need to use the same process for the Authorization to Return to Canada. Lastly, you must apply to the paper to the visa office responsible for your country.

WHAT TO CONSIDER IN ARC APPLICATION?

When you submit an ARC application you need to address the following issues:

- Explain why you received the removal order;
- why you may not repeat what caused the removal order in the first place;
- what are your reasons for returning to Canada;
- list any potential humanitarian and compassionate elements of your request; and
- why your reasons for returning to Canada overweigh the reasons for the initial removal order.

You sometimes need to address the root causes of the removal order, before or at the same time as applying for an ARC. For example, you may need to request rehabilitation or record suspension, if the inadmissibility is because of criminality. Consult with a competent professional for your options.

TIP # 75: CANADIAN IMMIGRATION COURTS AND ADMINISTRATIVE TRIBUNALS

Davit is an Armenian citizen. He became a permanent resident of Canada six year ago. Davit stayed in Canada for about one year but then left back because of his mother's illness. He took care of her ailing mother, but unfortunately, she died after several months of battle with her illness. Davit decided to go back to Canada after his mother's death. Since his PR card was not valid anymore, he applied for a PR Travel Document. An immigration officer refused his application because he did not meet the residency requirements. The refusal letter indicated he could file for an appeal to the Immigration and Refugee Board of Canada (IRB). David wonders what IRB is.

Immigration is an integral part of the Canadian legal system. The Immigration and Refugee Protection Act (IRPA) and the Immigration and Refugee Protection Regulations (IRPR) are the pillars of this system (see Tip # 8). They define the directions immigration officers and border services officers take in deciding on visa and immigration applications outside, at the time of entry and inside Canada.

Since the visa and immigration decisions affect people's lives, there are certain judicial options available in Canada to resolve refusals by the officers, objections to the decisions made by the officers, or decide whether a person may remain in Canada.

THE IMMIGRATION AND REFUGEE BOARD OF CANADA (IRB)

IRB is the largest administrative tribunal in Canada. It is very similar to a court, but it is less formal. IRB focuses on immigration and refugee matters only. The Immigration and Refugee Board of Canada consists of four divisions.

- The Immigration Division (ID),
- The Immigration Appeal Division (IAD),
- The Refugee Protection Division (RPD), and
- The Refugee Appeal Division (RAD).

THE IMMIGRATION DIVISION (ID)

The ID deals with two major matters: Admissibility to Canada and Detention Reviews

- **Admissibility to Canada** – Sections 33 to 43 of the IRPA lay out grounds of inadmissibility to Canada (see Tip # 81). The Immigration Division (ID) of the IRB holds admissibility hearings. CBSA usually refers people to the ID for such hearings. See Tip # 17 for the immigration acronyms.

- **Detention Review Hearings** – The CBSA detains foreign nationals and permanent residents in certain circumstances under provisions of the IRPA. The Immigration Division holds hearings within the first 48 hours of detention, then after seven days, and then every 30 days to decide whether the individual needs to remain in custody or not. Sometimes a bondsperson approaches the ID and posts a bond to encourage the Division to release the affected person under certain conditions.

THE IMMIGRATION APPEAL DIVISION (IAD)

The IAD holds the following hearings:

- **Appeals to the ID decisions** – If the ID deems a person inadmissible to Canada, they may have the option to appeal the decision to the IAD under subsections 63(2) and 63(3) of the IRPA. If the appeal is not available, they may file for Judicial Review to the Federal Court.

- **Appeals to the Sponsorship Applications Refusals** – If a Canadian Citizen or Permanent Resident sponsors a family member and an Immigration Officer refuses the application, they usually have the right to appeal the decision to the IAD under subsection 63(1) of the IRPA.

- **Appeals to termination of the Permanent Residency** – If an immigration officer decides a Permanent Resident has lost their permanent residency because they do not meet their residency obligations, the affected person may appeal this decision to the IAD under subsections 63(3) or 63(4) of the IRPA.

- **Appeals to visa or removal orders** – If a holder of a permanent residency visa or a protected person receives a removal order, they may appeal the decision to the IAD under subsection 63(2) of the IRPA.

- **Appeals by the Minister** – The Minister of Public Safety or the Minister of the Immigration, Refugees and Citizenship Canada may appeal the decisions of the ID to the IAD.

Under subsection 64(1) of the IRPA, there is no right to appeal for inadmissibility due to security, violating human or international rights, serious criminality or organized criminality. Also, subsection 64(3) of the IRPA prevents appeals to inadmissibility due to misrepresentation except for spouses and common-law partners in sponsorship applications.

THE REFUGEE PROTECTION DIVISION (RPD)

The RPD holds hearings for those who file for refugee protection under sections 96 and 97 of the IRPA. The hearings are for people who file for asylum either inside Canada or while entering Canada. Those who file for refugee status outside Canada will deal with the United Nations High Commissioner for Refugees (UNHCR) and then the Immigration, Refugees, and Citizenship Canada (IRCC) directly.

THE REFUGEE APPEAL DIVISION (RAD)

The RAD takes care of the appeals to the decisions made by the RPD under subsection 171 of the IRPA. Both the refugee claimant and the Minister may file for the appeal. The RAD usually does not hold oral hearings, but reviews written submissions of both parties and a panel of three members decides whether to allow or to dismiss the appeal.

THE FEDERAL COURT OF CANADA (FC)

Not every adverse decision by the immigration authorities give you the right to appeal the decision. Some examples of not-being-able-to-appeal situations include the following:

- Economic immigration applications such as the Express Entry, the Federal Self-employed class, the Provincial Nominee Programs, and the Start-up Visa.
- Temporary Resident Visa or Permit applications
- Authorization to Return to Canada (ARC) applications
- Rehabilitation applications
- Work Permit or Study Permit applications
- Permanent residency applications as caregivers or under the Humanitarian and Compassionate Considerations (H&C)

If an immigration officer refuses any of these applications or if your appeal to the IAD or the RAD is dismissed, you may have the opportunity to file for Judicial Review (JR) under section 72 of the IRPA.

The Federal Court of Canada holds Judicial Review hearings. If they allow the JR, the matter will go back to the immigration authorities or the IRB for a second review. Sometimes JR hearings are because the processing of the application has taken a long time.

OTHER COURTS

The Federal Court of Appeal (FCA) and the Supreme Court of Canada (SCC) may also deal with some immigration hearings.

Citizenship judges take care of the citizenship applications, and they may call the applicants for interviews, but the process is not a court-like process. While the citizenship judges are independent of the immigration authorities, they are not judicial officers.

TIP # 76: STAY BEYOND SIX MONTHS IN CANADA

Mohsen, an Iranian citizen, entered Canada as a tourist about five months ago. He currently stays with his brother who lives in Edmonton, Alberta. When Mohsen entered Canada, the Border Services Officer told him, he may stay in Canada for up to six months. However, he loves to stay beyond six months in Canada. He wonders if this is possible.

Canada welcomes millions of international tourists every year. For example, almost 21 million tourists visited Canada in 2017, about 14.3 million from the United States and 6.5 million from other countries[27]. To travel to Canada, a foreign national may need an eTA or a TRV. US citizens and some other people are exempt from both.

Regardless of their nationality, tourists may usually stay in Canada for up to six months. A Border Services Officer (BSO) has the final say in the length of stay for a foreign national, but they rarely limit the stay to less than six months or increase it beyond that.

Sometimes you decide to stay longer than six months in Canada. In these situations, you may have one or more of the following options after entering Canada.

APPLY FOR AN EXTENSION OF THE STAY

You need to apply for an extension of authorization to remain in Canada as a temporary resident before the expiry of your status. For example, if you enter Canada on the first day of February and the BSO does not impose any limitations to your stay, you need to submit your application before the end of July (note to practitioners – see section 181 of the IRPR). The immigration authorities recommend applying at least 30 days before the expiry of the status.

An immigration officer reviews your application, and if they believe you still meet the requirements of legal stay in Canada, they issue a Visitor Record. They mention the validity of your stay on the Visitor Record (i.e. an official document they mail to your address). A Visitor Record is not valid for re-entry to Canada.

The exact expiry date of the Visitor Record depends on the officer's decision, and it could be from a few days to a few months. I had clients who received a couple of weeks of extension and those who received up to 12 months. Of course, when you are applying for the extension, you need to mention for how long you want to stay. The officer usually considers your request.

You may request for the extension of the visitor record multiple times. However, the chances you get refused increases every time you apply for a new extension. The subsequently granted extensions are usually less than six months and could become limited to a few days only.

If you apply for an extension, but you do not receive the decision of the officer before the expiry of your current status, you do not need to panic. In this situation, you have an *implied status*. It means you are still a visitor. For example, if your status expires on August 1st and you apply in July, but the officer does not render a decision before August 1st, then you may continue staying in Canada until the officer renders their decision. If the decision is negative, you have to leave Canada immediately or apply for a Restoration of Status.

RESTORATION OF TEMPORARY RESIDENT STATUS

If your status in Canada expires and you do not have implied status, you need to either leave Canada immediately or apply for Restoration of Temporary Resident Status (note to practitioners – see section 182 of the

IRPR). While you are waiting for the outcome of this request, you have no status in Canada. The restoration process could take several weeks. If the officer refuses the application, you need to leave Canada immediately.

If the officer approves the application, you will receive a Visitor Record that shows the last day your status is valid.

APPLY FOR A WORK PERMIT OR A STUDY PERMIT

While you are in Canada as a visitor, you may not work or study, with the following exceptions:

- Working – If the work is exempt from a work permit (e.g. some performing artists or professional speakers and athletes) – See Tip # 48
- Working – For certain business visitors (note to practitioners – see section 187 of the IRPR) – See Tip # 60
- Studying – If the program is less than six months and it is not part of a longer program – See Tip # 63
- Studying – if the visitor is a minor child studying at a kindergarten, primary school, elementary school, or a secondary school only if their accompanying parents are permitted to work or study in Canada – See Tip # 70

Visitors may apply for a work permit or a study permit from inside Canada under the following circumstances.

- Study Permit (note to practitioners – see section 215 of the IRPR)
    - They are subject to an unenforceable removal order,
    - They are minor children who will be studying at the preschool, primary or secondary level,
    - They are visiting or exchange students who are studying at a designated learning institution,
    - They are accompanying family members of someone who holds a valid work permit or study permit,
    - They are accompanying family members of someone who holds a TRP that is valid for more than six months,
    - They are accompanying family members of certain

people who are exempt from work permits (e.g. they are accompanying a participant of sports activities or the employee of a foreign government),
- They have completed a course or program of study in Canada that is a prerequisite to their enrolling at a designated learning institution, or
- They submit their application to the Visa Application Centre in Los Angeles.

- Work Permit (note to practitioners – see sections 199, 206, and 207 of the IRPR)
  - They could work in Canada without a permit (except for business visitors) and now they want to work in a job that mandates a work permit,
  - Their permanent resident or citizen spouse or common-law partner has initiated their sponsorship application to Canada under the inside-Canada class,
  - They have applied for permanent residency under the Humanitarian and Compassionate (H&C) considerations, and their application has passed the first stage successfully,
  - They are a family member of the people described above,
  - They are subject to an unenforceable removal order,
  - They have made a claim for refugee protection that has been referred to the Refugee Protection Division but has not been determined,
  - They applied for a work permit before entering Canada, and the application was approved in writing, but they have not been issued the permit,
  - They hold a written statement from the Department of Foreign Affairs and International Trade stating that it has no objection to the foreign national working at a foreign mission in Canada, or
  - They are exempt under the USMCA (formerly NAFTA), or
  - They apply for a work permit by mail at the Visa Application Centre in New York.

As you can see this is a long list. You may, therefore, consider consulting with a professional for your options.

FILE FOR ASYLUM (REFUGEE CLAIM)

If you file a refugee claim, then the immigration officer issues you a removal order, but that removal order will not be enforceable until a final decision is made on your case. Therefore, you may stay in Canada for a few weeks or a few months longer.

Of course, if they approve your refugee claim, you may remain in Canada and apply for permanent residency. You need to have valid reasons for your refugee claim (e.g. being a convention refugee or a person who needs protection).

APPLY FOR PERMANENT RESIDENCY

Under certain programs, you may apply for the Permanent Residency of Canada and stay in our country while IRCC is processing your application. For example, you may apply for the Canadian Experience Class or the Caregiver programs inside Canada.

Note: This tip applies to visitors who are either US citizens or visiting Canada with a valid eTA or TRV. The article does not apply to TRP holders for the most part. See Tip # 79 about TRP and its potential options.

---

[27] https://globalnews.ca/news/4036090/canada-tourism-record-2017/

TIP # 77: DRIVING UNDER THE INFLUENCE

Yves is a citizen of Rwanda. He wants to travel to Canada next month to visit some family members. Yves knows that recreational cannabis is now legal in Canada. However, he wonders if there are some limitations. Yves does not want any trouble while he is in Canada.

Canada made significant changes to its DUI (Driving Under the Influence) regulations in December 2018. DUI include driving under the influence of alcohol (or rather drinking and driving), cannabis products (weed, marijuana, pot, joint, grass, edibles, etc.), or other drugs that alter your cognitive behaviour. Under the new law a DUI or rather impaired driving conviction could be serious criminality (see Tip # 81).

WHO WILL THE NEW LAW AFFECT?

The new DUI law affects the following people from an immigration standpoint:

- Permanent Residents of Canada
- International students
- Foreign workers

- Foreign visitors (tourists, international performing artists, international athletes, business visitors, etc.)
- Stateless or rather undocumented people
- Refugee claimants
- Other foreign nationals

Canadian citizens will also receive fines or jail time. They won't encounter immigration problems though. Canadian citizens have the unqualified right to enter and remain in Canada.

WHERE DOES THE OFFENCE NEED TO OCCUR?

The location of the offence is not important. Whether you receive a conviction in Canada or commit the offence outside Canada, you could still be inadmissible because of Driving Under the Influence.

WHAT DOES SERIOUS CRIMINALITY MEAN?

Serious criminality makes a person inadmissible to Canada. If you are outside Canada, you may not enter Canada. If you are inside Canada, you will lose your status in Canada and will receive a deportation order. Also, most people who receive removal orders due to serious criminality has no right to appeal.

WHAT CAN YOU DO ABOUT INADMISSIBILITY DUE TO A DUI CONVICTION?

You could fight your removal order at an IRB hearing, but if you fail or if you are already outside Canada, you could seek one of the following potential remedies.

- If you completed your sentence less than five years ago, you need to apply for a Temporary Resident Permit (TRP). Of course, TRP is a temporary remedy, but if you are successful, you may enter and remain in Canada for up to three years.

- If you completed your sentence more than five years ago, then you could apply for Rehabilitation. The rehabilitation process is complex, but if you succeed, the immigration authorities clear your name. In other words, you could potentially travel or immigrate to Canada like a person who is not inadmissible to Canada.
- Sometimes you need to apply for an ARC (see Tip # 74)

The information I have presented here is generic and may differ from case to case.

TIP # 78: FIVE OPTIONS TO VISA OR IMMIGRATION APPLICATIONS REFUSALS

Alsu is a citizen of Uzbekistan. She applied for immigration to Canada under the Express Entry system. Alsu, unfortunately, received a refusal letter two weeks ago. She is confident the immigration officer has made a mistake. Alsu wants to go to the court and revive her application.

Sometimes the immigration authorities refuse your application. Refusal is hurtful, but you could do something about it. This article shows some potential options to you, depending on what application you submitted and why they refused it.

OPTION #1 – APPEAL THE DECISION

Under certain circumstances, you may appeal the decision of the officer to the Immigration Appeal Division (IAD) of the Immigration and Refugee Board of Canada (IRB). Section 63 of the Immigration and Refugee Protection Act (IRPA) lists these circumstances as follows:

- Refused sponsorship applications for spouses or children, parents, or other family members

- Removal orders due to inadmissibility or due to not meeting the residency requirements of permanent residency
- Removal orders for permanent resident visa holders
- Refusing a PR travel document to a permanent resident of Canada

There is no right to appeal for inadmissibility due to security, violating human or international rights, serious criminality, organized criminality, or misrepresentation. Spouses and children are exempt from the misrepresentation prohibition, and they may still appeal the decision of the immigration officer.

There is no right to appeal for other applications such as Temporary Resident Visas (TRV), Express Entry applications, Temporary Resident Permits (TRP), or Provincial Nominee Programs (PNP).

If you do not have the right to appeal, you could have the right to Judicial Review. If the IAD allows your appeal, they approve it immediately (with some exceptions). If the IAD refuses your appeal, you could have the right to file for a Judicial Review.

OPTION #2 – JUDICIAL REVIEW

If you have no right to appeal or the IAD refuses your appeal, you could file for Judicial Review under section 72 of the IRPA. The authority that reviews such applications is the Federal Court of Canada. The Judicial Review process usually consists of two steps.

- **Step 1 – an Application for Leave for Judicial Review**: Your lawyer will submit a request to the court and asks for Judicial Review. If the court accepts the request, your case will be heard by the court at an oral hearing.
- **Step 2 – an Oral Hearing**: The judge hears both sides of the story and decides whether to vote in your favour or not. If they do, your case will be returned to the immigration authorities for a fair review.

Unlike the appeal hearings, even if you win a judicial review case, you may still get refused by the immigration authorities. The odds will be in your favour for sure, but there is no guarantee for success. The Judicial Review process could review the errors of the officer in fact or law. It also considers procedural fairness or rather whether the application was processed fairly and in a timely fashion.

OPTION #3 – REQUEST FOR RECONSIDERATION

You may contact the immigration officer via the IRCC Web Form or email and request for reconsideration. When you submit such requests make sure to consider the following:

- Be courteous to the immigration officer
- Be clear about your request
- Explain why you believe you deserve reconsideration
- Present any documents that support your request
- Refer to the potential Humanitarian and Compassionate elements of your request (e.g. the hardship you are facing, and the best interests of a child affected by the decision of the officer)

Immigration officers tend to ignore the majority of requests for reconsideration, but if it goes through, they may decide to reopen your case.

OPTION 4 – CONSIDER ALTERNATIVE OPTIONS

Sometimes alternative options could be available to you. For example,

- Apply for a TRP if the refusal of the application is due to inadmissibility
- Apply for a record suspension if you are inadmissible to Canada because of a criminal record in Canada
- Apply for rehabilitation if you are inadmissible due to criminal record outside Canada (certain limitations apply)
- Apply for an Authorization to Return to Canada (ARC) if you have received an Exclusion or a Deportation order
- File for a pre-removal risk assessment in case your refugee claim is refused (certain limitations apply)
- Apply under the Humanitarian and Compassionate (H&C) considerations, if there is a basis for H&C (e.g. the best interests of a child)
- Apply for another method of immigration (e.g. Express Entry

instead of sponsorship). Of course, you need to meet the requirements of the alternative method.

You may consult with a Regulated Canadian Immigration Consultant (RCIC) or an immigration lawyer for your potential alternatives.

OPTION # 5 – APPLY AGAIN

If the refusal is not because of inadmissibility or misrepresentation, you could apply again. However, do it so if you either have new evidence to offer or your circumstances have changed significantly. Make sure to address the previous officer's concerns in your new application.

TIP # 79: TRP – TEMPORARY RESIDENT PERMIT TO CANADA

Mike is an American citizen. He has been a law-abiding citizen all his life. However, he ran over a pedestrian in Seattle three years ago. His blood alcohol level was two times more than the legal limit. The judge convicted Mike of driving under the influence (DUI) resulting in bodily harm. He served 90 days in prison. Mike also had to do community service for one year.

He completed his sentence and community service more than a year ago. Mike wants to visit his ailing mother who lives in Regina, Saskatchewan. His mother suffers from a terminal disease and currently spends her last days at a local hospice. Mike knows he is inadmissible to Canada, but he wonders if he could obtain a Temporary Resident Permit (TRP) and comfort her mother in her last days.

Sometimes a person becomes inadmissible to Canada due to misrepresentation or other reasons such as criminality, security, or medical issues (see Tip # 81). One of the potential remedies to inadmissibility is receiving a Temporary Resident Permit (TRP) from the Canadian immigration authorities (the IRCC).

WHAT IS TRP?

TRP is permission to stay in Canada for a limited period. A TRP could be valid for one day and up to three years. TRP does not allow you to cross a port of entry or board an airplane that is destined to Canada. As a result, if you are outside Canada and an immigration officer approves your request, they may issue an eTA or a TRV for you, depending on your nationality (the US Citizens are exempt from eTA or TRV and do not need extra documents).

You are subject to examination at the port of entry and a Border Services Officer (BSO) decides whether to let you enter Canada or not. If you are already inside Canada and they approve your TRP, you do not need to leave the country, and you may stay for as long as the TRP is valid.

HOW TO GET A TRP?

The application for TRP is similar to an application for a Temporary Resident Visa (TRV). However, you have to consider the following:

- Apply in the paper to the appropriate visa office responsible for your country of nationality or residence,
- request for a TRP,
- include all the reasons you believe make you eligible for a TRP,
- include documents related to your inadmissibility,
- pay the processing fee of $200 (some applicants are exempt from the fee, such as those inadmissible under criminality or rather subsection 36(2) of the IRPA).

The officer considers several factors to make sure your reasons for entering Canada outweigh the inadmissibility, for example:

- Your family ties in Canada,
- humanitarian and compassionate reasons,
- the reasons behind inadmissibility,
- your history,
- the credibility of your claims,
- potential controversies,
- the potential use of social assistance in Canada,

- eligibility for a record suspension or rehabilitation,
- and previous removals from Canada).

THE BENEFITS OF A TRP

If you receive a TRP you could enjoy the following benefits (subject to approval by an immigration officer):

- You may stay in Canada for as long as the TRP is valid unless changes to your circumstances invalidate the TRP
- If the TRP is valid for six months or more, you may apply for a Work Permit or a Study Permit and then work or study in Canada
- If the inadmissibility is due to a family member or because of the health grounds and you continuously stay in Canada with valid TRPs for at least three years, you could apply for Permanent Residency of Canada (note to practitioners: see paragraph 65(b)(i) of the IRPR).
- If the inadmissibility is due to criminality (or rather subsection 36(1) of the IRPA), and you continuously stay in Canada with valid TRPs for at least five years, you could apply for Permanent Residency of Canada (note to practitioners: see paragraph 65(b)(ii) of the IRPR)

To be eligible to apply for permanent residency, you need to stay in Canada continuously. Therefore, you need to apply for multiple TRPs, and each time show to the officer you meet the requirements.

WHO MAY NOT APPLY FOR A TRP?

If someone claims refugee status in Canada, they may not apply for a TRP within the 12 months following the refusal, withdrawal, or abandonment of the refugee claim. If that person files for a TRP after the 12-month ban, the officer ignores the reasons for the refugee claim (i.e. sections 96 and 97 of the IRPA), and only focuses on the merits of the request for a TRP.

WHAT IS THE VALIDITY OF A TRP?

As I mentioned earlier, the validity of a TRP could be between one day and three years (note to practitioners – see section 63 of the IRPR). An immigration officer or a CBSA officer may cancel the TRP at any time.

If you leave Canada, the TRP becomes invalid. Under special circumstances, an immigration officer may issue a TRP which is valid for re-entry. However, this is quite uncommon, so do not count on it. In other words, TRP usually remains valid for as long as you stay in Canada and it has not reached the expiry date. If you are still in Canada and your TRP will expire soon, you may apply for a new TRP, but you have to go through the same process (i.e. submitting all the forms, documents, and the processing fee).

TIP # 80: MISREPRESENTATION

Isla is a citizen of Mali. She hid an important document from the immigration officer while she was applying for a study permit to Canada. The immigration officer found out and refused Isla's application. They also sent her a letter which indicated she was inadmissible to Canada because of misrepresentation. She wonders what the implications of the letter are. Isla wants to know about potential remedies to this situation.

When you apply for immigration, visa, study permit, or work permit to Canada you need to answer several questions. You also need to submit several documents. The questions and documents reveal the following:

- Your identity (name, date of birth, citizenship, etc.)
- Your marital status (single, married, common-law relationships, etc.)
- Your family members (dependent or non-dependent; accompanying or non-accompanying)
- Your background (criminal, security, medical, etc.)
- Your suitability for the method of visa or application you are applying (e.g. education, financial status, work history, funds available to you, work status, etc.)

- Other (e.g. your ties to your home country or Canada)

The exact questions depend on the type of application and in some cases your country of origin.

MATERIAL FACT AND MISREPRESENTATION

The information that affects the decision of the immigration officer is a material fact. You must share the material fact with the officer thoroughly and without altering. If you knowingly withhold the material fact from the officer or make changes to it, then you have committed misrepresentation. You may do so directly or indirectly. Regardless, misrepresentation applies to you. Some examples of misrepresentation include:

- Hiding material fact from the immigration officer
- Forge documents
- Report figures, dates, amounts, addresses, and names incorrectly

If the mistakes do not affect the application or if you make them unknowingly, the officer could ignore misrepresentation.

THE CONSEQUENCES OF MISREPRESENTATION

The Immigration and Refugee Protection Act (IRPA) is harsh to those who commit misrepresentation. Under section 40 of the IRPA, a foreign national or a permanent resident will be inadmissible to Canada for five years due to misrepresentation. It is obvious the officer refuses the application as well. In the case of permanent residents of Canada, they will lose their permanent residency and become foreign nationals concerning Canada (see Tip # 7).

Section 40 of the IRPA does not affect Canadian citizens. However, if the misrepresentation had occurred when they were applying for citizenship or when they were applying for permanent residency, they could lose their Canadian citizenship under section 10 of the Citizenship Act.

Under section 127 of the IRPA, any person who undermines the Immigration and Refugee Protection Act by misrepresentation has committed an offence. Misrepresentation in this context includes withholding or altering material facts or refusing to answer the questions raised by an officer or affirm the truthfulness of their answers. Under section 126 of the IRPA, those who help the applicant commit misrepresentation also commit an offence. Under section 128 of the IRPA, if your actions fall under sections 126 or 127 of the IRPA, you may face up to five years imprisonment or up to $100,000 fine or a combination of both. Remember that sections 126 to 128 of the IRPA apply to foreign nationals, permanent residents of Canada, and Canadian citizens alike.

If you misrepresent, you lose the right to appeal the decision made by the officer except for spouses or common-law partners in sponsorship applications (see subsection 64(3) of the IRPA).

REMEDY FOR MISREPRESENTATION

If an officer considers you inadmissible to Canada due to misrepresentation, you might have the following options within the first five years of being banned from Canada.

- Challenge the decision to the Federal Court (i.e. Judicial Review)
- Apply for an Authorization to Return to Canada if you have received an Exclusion Order due to misrepresentation
- Apply for a Temporary Resident Permit to be able to come back to Canada for a limited period

If five years passes from inadmissibility, you may apply for visa or immigration to Canada. Expect the officers to scrutinize your application though.

CONCLUSION

Make sure you understand what material fact is. Be truthful and do not hide the material fact from the immigration officers or border services officers. The consequences are significant. Of course, if the facts are irrelevant to the application and do not affect the decision of the officer in any shape and form, you are not obliged to share them with the officer. The rule of thumb says everything on the forms and document checklists is a material fact. Sometimes you make mistakes and officers consider them as misrepresentation. You need to communicate the matter with the officer as soon as you can and do your best to convince them you did not misrepresent.

TIP # 81: WHO IS INADMISSIBLE TO CANADA?

Jalal is a citizen of Afghanistan. He intends to immigrate to Canada under the Express Entry system. Jalal had a clash with the law when he was 16 years old. He stole some money from his school. Jalal never served prison time, but despite being 25, his police report reflects the issue. Jalal wonders if he is inadmissible to Canada.

Canada has strict rules to protect the safety and security of its citizens and the integrity of its immigration system. As a result, certain people may be inadmissible to Canada.

WHAT DOES INADMISSIBILITY TO CANADA MEAN?

If a person is inadmissible to Canada and lives outside the country may not visit, study, work or immigrate to Canada. If an inadmissible person is currently inside Canada, has to leave Canada immediately.

WHO DO INADMISSIBILITY RULES AFFECT?

All of the inadmissibility rules affect foreign nationals. Some of these rules affect Permanent Residents of Canada (i.e. people who have already immigrated to Canada but are not naturalized citizens yet). The inadmissibility rules do not affect Canadian citizens as they have the unqualified right to enter and remain in Canada under the Constitution Act, 1982.

UNDER WHAT CIRCUMSTANCES, A PERSON BECOMES INADMISSIBLE TO CANADA?

The following table shows the causes of inadmissibility (see sections 33 to 43 of the Immigration and Refugee Protection Act). In this table, PR means Permanent Residents and FN means Foreign Nationals.

Type	Examples	Who
Security	Espionage, Subversion of a Government by Force, Terrorism, Danger to the Security of Canada, etc.	PR, FN
Human or international rights violations	Crimes Against Humanity and War Crimes	PR, FN
Serious criminality	Committing a crime that the maximum term of imprisonment is at least ten years or the actual term of imprisonment is more than six months	PR, FN
Criminality	Indictable offences, etc.	FN
Organized criminality	Being a member of a criminal gang	PR, FN
Health grounds	A danger to public health or safety or causing excessive demand to the Universal Healthcare system in Canada	FN
Financial reasons	Not being able to support themselves in Canada	FN

Type	Examples	Who
Misrepresentation	Misrepresenting or withholding material facts	PR, FN
Non-compliance with the Act	Several reasons such as a PR not meeting the residency requirements or FN studies in Canada without a valid Study Permit	PR, FN

HOW TO RESOLVE INADMISSIBILITY?

Depending on the nature of the inadmissibility and whether the affected person is in Canada or not, they could have one or more of these options. In some cases, none of the options are available.

- Attending a hearing at the Immigration Division (ID) of the Immigration Refugee Board of Canada (IRB)
- Appealing the decision of the immigration officer or the ID at the Immigration Appeal Division of the IRB
- Filing for Judicial Review with the Federal Court of Canada
- Requesting Rehabilitation from the IRCC to remove the inadmissibility forever
- Requesting a Temporary Resident Permit (TRP) to be able to enter or stay in Canada despite the inadmissibility
- Applying for a Declaration of Relief under subsection 42.1(1) of the IRPA for inadmissibility to Canada under section 34 (security), paragraphs 35(1)(b) or (c) (human or international rights violations), or subsection 37(1) (organized criminality) of the IRPA
- Requesting permanent residency of Canada under the Humanitarian and Compassionate Considerations
- In the case of inadmissibility due to misrepresentation, waiting for five years

TIP # 82: MEDICAL INADMISSIBILITY TO CANADA

Faten is a citizen of Saudi Arabia. She is in the process of immigration to Canada. Faten's new husband is a Canadian citizen. To live together, he has sponsored her to Canada. Faten recently went through a medical examination and realized she has type 2 diabetes. Consequently, she wonders if the disease prevents her from immigrating to Canada and joining her husband. Is Faten inadmissible to Canada?

One of the objectives of the Canadian immigration system is to protect the safety and health of Canadians. As a result, if you want to immigrate to Canada, you need to show to an immigration officer, you are not inadmissible to our country because of medical issues.

WHICH MEDICAL ISSUES DO MAKE YOU INADMISSIBLE TO CANADA?

Under section 38 of the Immigration and Refugee Protection Act (IRPA), you could become inadmissible because of one of the following reasons.

- You are likely to be a danger to the health of Canadians

- You are likely to be a danger to the safety of Canadians
- Your health conditions may cause excessive demand on health or social services

A DANGER TO PUBLIC HEALTH

At the moment, IRCC considers the following a danger to the public health of Canadians:

- Active pulmonary tuberculosis (TB)
- Untreated syphilis

They find people with these conditions inadmissible to Canada. Therefore, if you are suffering from any of these conditions, seek medical treatment before applying for immigration to Canada.

Also, if you are suffering from any severe contagious disease, make sure to treat it first. Keep in mind that IRCC may issue a temporary ban on immigration for certain people or specific regions of the world because of the outbreak of serious illnesses. For example, we have had advisories and bans on Ebola and Avian influenza (Bird flu) in the past.

A DANGER TO PUBLIC SAFETY

Persons who could endanger the safety of Canadians could become inadmissible to Canada. Some examples include the following:

- certain impulsive sociopathic behaviour disorders;
- some aberrant sexual disorders such as pedophilia;
- certain paranoid states or some organic brain syndromes associated with violence or risk of harm to others;
- applicants with substance abuse leading to antisocial behaviours such as violence, and impaired driving; and
- other types of hostile, disruptive behaviour[28].

This list is just for guidance. The officers review applications on a case by case basis.

CAUSING EXCESSIVE DEMAND

If your health condition results in any of the following, you may not immigrate to Canada:

- Increasing the medical wait time of the Canadians to the point that the rate of mortality or morbidity increases, or
- putting a significant strain on the amount of money the Canadian universal healthcare system has to spend for you.

You may ask what does significant strain mean? The current figure is an amount of $19,812 per year (subject to change). The officers usually consider five years for their calculations. In other words, if your expenses exceed $99,060 for five years from the time you enter Canada, then you may become inadmissible. Honestly, I simplified the matter as much as I could, but when it comes to the excessive demand, the calculations and factors you need to consider are a lot more complicated than this.

EXEMPTIONS

Nobody is exempt from the danger to public health and safety provisions, but the following people are exempt from the excessive demand:

- Spouses or common-law partners in sponsorship applications only,
- children or adopted children in sponsorship applications only,
- convention refugees or people in need of protection, or
- spouses, common-law partners, or children of the people mentioned above

WHO DOES CONDUCT MEDICAL EXAMINATIONS?

A panel physician conducts medical examinations. A typical medical exam consists of an interview, physical examination, laboratory tests, and chest x-ray. Depending on your health conditions and the type of your application, the scope of a medical exam could change. The IRCC website posts the list of panel physicians. The following link redirects you the relevant page:

settler.ca/88/panel

The panel physician uploads your information to a secure website. A medical officer reviews the report and then informs your immigration officer whether you pass the medical examination or not. If you pass, they issue you a medical certificate, but they usually do not share it with you. The immigration officer may request further tests or send you a procedural fairness letter.

WHAT IS A PROCEDURAL FAIRNESS LETTER?

If you receive a procedural fairness letter, it means the officer suspects or believes you are inadmissible to Canada because of medical issues. If you agree with them, you may not immigrate to Canada. However, you could fight back. Consult with a professional if you have received a procedural fairness letter. Don't take this matter lightly.

MEDICAL EXAMINATION FOR TEMPORARY STATUS

Immigration officers may request medical tests for temporary cases as well. For example, you may receive a medical examination request for your TRV (visitor's visa), TRP, Study Permit, or Work Permit applications. Generally speaking, most people do not receive such correspondences, but if you do you have to comply.

If you do not go through a medical examination for your work permit, then you may face limitations. For example, you may not work in:

- childcare services,
- healthcare services,
- primary or secondary schools, and
- farming industry if you are from certain countries.

If you are also from certain countries and you want to work for more than six months in Canada, you need to go through the medical examination.

MEDICAL SURVEILLANCE

Sometimes the officers allow you to enter Canada but ask you to go through medical surveillance. In other words, you need to introduce yourself to the healthcare authorities of your province of destination. Then they will examine you every now and again. The surveillance is usually every six months for five years or so.

OVERCOMING MEDICAL INADMISSIBILITY

If you receive a procedural fairness letter you may try to fight back, but if you fail, you may consider the following solutions:

- Immigration to Canada under Humanitarian and Compassionate considerations (H&C) – See Tip # 47
- Receiving a Temporary Resident Permit (TRP) – See Tip # 79

---

[28] https://www.canada.ca/en/immigration-refugees-citizenship/corporate/publications-manuals/operational-bulletins-manuals/standard-requirements/medical-requirements/refusals-inadmissibility/danger-public-health-public-safety.html

PART SIX:
SETTLING IN CANADA

TIP # 83: CANADA DAY – A REMINDER OF CANADIAN CITIZENSHIP

Draen immigrated to Canada from Croatia two years ago. He is excited to become a Canadian citizen soon. Although Draen is not a Canadian citizen yet, he celebrates Canada Day on July first every year. He considers himself a Canadian already.

Canada Day marks the inception of Canada on July 1, 1867, when the Constitution Act, 1867 (also known as the British North America Act, 1867) came into effect. However, it took us several years to claim our full sovereignty and identity as a country. For example, Canadian Citizenship as we know it came to existence only on January 1, 1947.

WHO IS A CANADIAN CITIZEN?

The Canadian Citizenship Act has gone through many changes since its initial introduction in 1947. The current version defines a citizen under sections 3 to 5 of the Act. If I simplify the provisions of the Act, Canadian Citizenship is boiled down to the following categories.

- Any person who is born in Canada (except those born to foreign diplomats)

- A first-generation Canadian who is born outside Canada
- A person who immigrates to Canada and then later becomes a naturalized citizen

The categories that I explained above are very generic. There are many exceptions to this list. Explaining them is beyond the scope of this book.

WHO IS A NATURALIZED CITIZEN?

People may immigrate to Canada under three main categories of Family Reunification, Economic Immigration, and Refugees. When a person immigrates to Canada, they become Permanent Residents of Canada. These Permanent Residents may become Canadian Citizens if they meet certain criteria, such as:

- Have been physically present in Canada for at least 1095 days in the past five years as a permanent resident of Canada. They may also receive credit for being present in Canada as a visitor, international student, or foreign worker.
- Their permanent residency is valid and not under review.
- They do not face a removal order from Canada.
- They have filed their taxes regularly (at least three times in the past five years).
- They know one of the official languages of Canada (i.e. French or English).
- They do not face major issues with the law inside or outside Canada.

The list I have presented is very broad. For specific criteria, you may consult the IRCC website or a Canadian Citizenship Professional.

If someone meets the requirements, they need to apply for Citizenship, pass the Citizenship test (depending on their age), and take the Citizenship Oath.

Here is the oath of Canadian citizenship in English:

> I swear (or affirm) that I will be faithful and bear true allegiance to Her Majesty Queen Elizabeth the Second, Queen of Canada, Her Heirs and Successors, and that I will faithfully observe the laws of Canada and fulfil my duties as a Canadian citizen.

And, here is the oath of Canadian citizenship in French:

> Je jure (ou j'affirme solennellement) Que je serai fidèle Et porterai sincère allégeance à Sa Majesté la Reine Elizabeth Deux Reine du Canada À ses héritiers et successeurs Que j'observerai fidèlement les lois du Canada Et que je remplirai loyalement mes obligations de citoyen canadien.

People who successfully meet all the requirements, eventually take the Citizenship Oath to become *naturalized citizens*. The rules and regulations of Canada are the same for born citizens and naturalized citizens. When you become a naturalized citizen, nobody can take citizenship away from you, unless you have obtained your citizenship or permanent residency fraudulently.

WHO IS A FIRST-GENERATION CANADIAN?

A first-generation Canadian concerning the Citizenship Act is someone who is born outside Canada, but at least one of their parents is either a naturalized citizen or a citizen who is born inside Canada. A first-generation Canadian is a Canadian citizen by birth.

CANADIAN PASSPORT

When you become a Canadian Citizen, you may apply for a Canadian passport. However, you need to meet certain criteria and, in most cases, have a guarantor. Some non-citizens of Canada may also be eligible for Canadian passports or rather travel documents under certain circumstances.

TIP # 84: CANADIAN BANKS AND CREDIT UNIONS

Grace is a Togolese citizen who has recently immigrated to Canada. She landed in Fredericton, New Brunswick, a couple of days ago. Since Grace brought seven thousand dollars with her to the country, she wants to open an account as soon as possible. She wants to know about the most reliable banks in Canada. Moreover, Grace has heard Canadian banks charge bank fees. She wonders what those are.

The Canadian financial system consists of a complex network of institutions. Banks are at the centre point of this system. However, there are many other financial institutions such as credit unions that help people with their financial needs. For example, think about having a personal chequing or savings account, a business account, personal or business loans, mortgages for purchasing houses, and more.

While there are several banks in Canada, five of them handle most of the financial matters in Canada.

THE "BIG FIVE" BANKS

The term "Big Five" refers to these banks:

- Canadian Imperial Bank of Commerce (CIBC)
- Bank of Montreal (BMO)
- Toronto-Dominion Bank (TD)
- Bank of Nova Scotia (Scotiabank)
- Royal Bank of Canada (RBC)

These five banks are the largest banks in Canada. Consequently, they handle most of the financial transactions in Canada.

OTHER BANKS – SECOND-TIER BANKS

You may need to know many other Canadian banks are quite large but not as large as the Big Five. Here are some examples.

- National Bank of Canada (NBC)
- HSBC Bank Canada
- Canadian Western Bank
- Tangerine Bank
- Laurentian Bank

OTHER FINANCIAL INSTITUTIONS

Some financial institutions in Canada may offer limited banking options such as loans and mortgages. For example, take a look at these institutions:

- Desjardins
- Citi Group Canada

CREDIT UNIONS

Credit unions are financial co-operatives. It means you need to be a member to open an account with them. As a member, you share the profit of the Credit Union at the end of their fiscal years. Credit unions are usually local. In other words, they usually operate in a couple of cities or provinces only. If you want to know more about credit unions visit the Canadian Credit Unions Association website.

BANK FEES

Canadian banks rarely offer free services to their clients. Welcome to Canada!

Some of the potential bank fees include fixed monthly fees and withdrawal fees. Furthermore, they may even charge you for cheque or cash deposits. When you open an account with a bank, make sure you know the potential bank fees. Therefore, compare the fees with other options the banks offer and pick the best one.

TIP # 85: VOCATIONAL TRAINING IN ONTARIO

Eddy is a Citizen of Guatemala. He intends to study in Canada. Eddy has heard Ontario is the most populated province of Canada. Since he prefers to see many people around him, he has decided to pick a career college in Ontario. Eddy wants to become an accountant. He is looking for a two-year accounting diploma that can help him land a good job in the future.

Ontario is the second largest province of Canada regarding the area and the largest province concerning the population. Two out of every five Canadians live in Ontario. Education is an integral part of this province. Vocational training refers to those educational programs that help you find a job. Four different types of institutions offer vocational training in the province of Ontario.

- Universities
- Community Colleges
- Private Career Colleges
- Private Training Institutes

ONTARIO UNIVERSITIES

The main focus of Ontario Universities is undergraduate or postgraduate programs. They usually offer programs which lead to receiving a bachelor's degree, a master's degree, or a Ph.D. Many universities also offer certificate or diploma programs that are job-oriented. In this sense, the university acts as a vocational institute. The programs vary and could be full-time or part-time, undergraduate or postgraduate, online or on campus, and result in a certificate or degree. Sometimes a university offers vocational seminars and crash courses to help professionals enhance their job knowledge and capabilities.

When you sign up with a university for a vocational program, remember that you may not have chosen the most cost-effective option. Shop around and see if you can find similar programs offered by other institutes with the same quality but less expensive.

COMMUNITY COLLEGES

Community colleges or rather "Colleges of Applied Arts and Technology" are partly funded by the government of Ontario. Therefore, their services are very cost-effective for local students. The main focus of community colleges is vocational training. They usually offer certificate or diploma programs that build up skills to do a specific job. For example, if you want to become a computer programmer, a mechanic, an accountant, or a chef, you may consider attending one of these colleges.

According to the Ontario Ministry of Training, Colleges, and Universities, there are currently 24 community colleges active in Ontario. These colleges spread in different parts of the province. Two of them are French-language colleges. Many of them have more than one campus locations which extend their services to more than one city or region. They also offer online programs as well.

Considering the expertise of community colleges in vocational training and relatively affordable tuition, I strongly recommend considering their programs before looking into other options. Many of these colleges offer affordable housing for those students who come from out of town.

Here is a list of existing community colleges in Ontario.

College Name	Main Campus City
Algonquin College of Applied Arts and Technology	Nepean
Cambrian College of Applied Arts and Technology	Sudbury
Canadore College of Applied Arts and Technology	North Bay
Centennial College	Toronto
Collège Boréal	Sudbury
Conestoga College Institute of Technology	Kitchener
Confederation College of Applied Arts and Technology	Thunder Bay
Durham College of Applied Arts and Technology	Oshawa
Fanshawe College of Applied Arts and Technology	London
Fleming College	Peterborough
George Brown College of Applied Arts and Technology	Toronto
Georgian College of Applied Arts and Technology	Barrie
Humber College Institute of Technology and Advanced Learning	Toronto
La Cité collégiale	Ottawa
Lambton College of Applied Arts and Technology	Sarnia
Loyalist College of Applied Arts and Technology	Belleville
Mohawk College of Applied Arts and Technology	Hamilton
Niagara College of Applied Arts and Technology	Welland
Northern College of Applied Arts and Technology	Timmins
St. Clair College of Applied Arts and Technology	Windsor
St. Lawrence College of Applied Arts and Technology	Kingston
Sault College	Sault Ste. Marie
Seneca College of Applied Arts and Technology	North York
Sheridan College Institute of Technology and Advanced Learning	Oakville

PRIVATE CAREER COLLEGES

As the name suggests, Private Career Colleges (PCC) are independent of the government. In other words, such colleges cover most or all of their costs through tuition fees.

Attending a private career college is probably the least cost-effective option. However, they usually tend to offer training that is not offered by community colleges. They also offer expedited training. For example, you may receive a diploma in less than one year compared to two or three-year programs by community colleges. Many PCCs offer the latest technical training and skills that could lead you to get the job you deserve.

There is some government funding available for those who have lost their jobs. If you are eligible for such funds, then you may be lucky to attend a PCC without paying a penny. Also, the Ontario Student Assistance Program (OSAP) may cover some PCC programs. OSAP offers grants and loans for higher education.

Private Career Colleges (PCC) need to offer accredited programs, meaning that the Ontario Ministry of Training, Colleges, and Universities certifies their programs. When you sign up with a PCC make sure this is true about the program. Sometimes they offer programs that are pending approval, and you may end up spending several months and thousands of dollars to receive a non-accredited certificate.

PRIVATE TRAINING INSTITUTES

These types of institutions offer non-accredited career-booster programs. Most of their programs are in the form of short-term courses. Sometimes they are affiliated with large corporations and offer certificates that are approved by them.

TIP # 86: SAMPLE CANADIAN RESUMES

Susan recently lost her good-paying job at an auto-making plant in southern Ontario. She is looking for a job, but her advisor told her she needs to revise her resume.

Resume or rather Résumé (also known as CV or curriculum vitae) is usually the first document you submit to an employer when you apply for a job. Whether your resume includes a cover letter or not, it plays an important role in the employment process.

This Tip leads you to some sample resumes in the preferred Canadian formats.

CHRONOLOGICAL RESUME

A chronological resume is the most common format in Canada. It highlights your work experience. A chronological resume presents the experience in reverse chronological order. In other words, you specify your latest role first. This type of resume is useful when you seek a job relevant to your work experience. Visit the following link for a sample chronological resume:

settler.ca/88/chr

FUNCTIONAL RESUME (SKILLS RESUME)

If you are pursuing a career that is not much dependent on your experience, then you need to highlight your skills and education. Functional resumes also known as Skills resumes are ideal for such situations. New college or university graduates may also consider this type of resume to find a job. Visit the following link for a sample functional resume:

settler.ca/88/fun

COMBINATION RESUME

A combination resume is nothing but a combination of both skills and work experience. Visit the following link for a sample combination resume:

settler.ca/88/com

Sometimes you might need to submit a Detailed Resume. Such resumes are similar to combination resumes, but you need to explain every achievement or duty in detail. A detailed resume may be several pages. However, a typical resume is usually two or fewer pages.

Some relevant Tips:

- Tip # 54: Job Search Websites in Canada
- Tip # 55: Cold Calling for Job Search

TIP # 87: SOCIAL INSURANCE NUMBER

Logan is from Falkland Islands (Islas Malvinas). He landed in Canada as a newcomer a few weeks ago. The border officer handed Logan a nine-digit number. She told him, the number represents his SIN. Logan has no idea what the use of SIN is.

Every person who wants to work in Canada or benefit from certain government services needs a Social Insurance Number (SIN). This number consists of 9 digits.

WHO CAN HAVE A SOCIAL INSURANCE NUMBER?

If you are a Canadian citizen or a Permanent Resident (PR) of Canada, then you are entitled to receive a SIN. Certain temporary residents such as foreign workers and international students receive SIN too. If you do not have a SIN, then you cannot work in Canada. However, being in the position of a SIN does not mean you can work in Canada. If you are not a Canadian citizen or PR, then you usually need a valid work permit to work.

All employers ask for your Social Insurance Number during the hiring process. If your visa does not qualify you for a SIN then you are not able to work in Canada (i.e. any type of work such as full-time, part-time, contract, temporary, and casual).

Children who are 12 years or older may directly apply for a SIN. Parents or guardians of children under 12 may apply for a SIN on their behalf. A SIN is mandatory to receive a government grant under the RESP program[29]. There may also be some other services that request for a Social Insurance Number. The sooner you get the SIN for your children, the better.

SOCIAL INSURANCE NUMBER IS UNIQUE

Every person in Canada owns a unique Social Insurance Number. In other words, every SIN belongs to one person only. Therefore, you cannot share your SIN with others. Since SIN is attached to your identity, it is important to protect it. Share your Social Insurance Number only with those whom you trust. If you own a SIN card, do not to carry it in your wallet[30].

In case of theft, a SIN is the best tool for wrong-doers to access your identity and commit identity theft. If somebody manages to access your identity, they may empty your bank accounts, abuse your credit cards, get loans on your behalf, and even put you into more serious troubles such as criminal accusations.

WHO DOES ISSUE SIN?

Service Canada is a federal government organization that issues Social Insurance Numbers. You may refer to any Service Canada centre to request a Social Insurance Number. They usually issue the number immediately. When you immigrate to Canada, you usually receive your SIN at the time of landing.

---

[29] RESP stands for Registered Educational Savings Program. It financially assists students pursue higher education.
[30] The government does not issue SIN cards anymore.

TIP # 88: CANADA SALES TAXES - GST, PST, RST, AND HST

Johana is a tourist from French Guiana. She is currently visiting Vancouver, British Columbia. Johana is a bit confused at the time of shopping. The amount that she pays for the items she purchases is different from the posted price. For example, the price tag of an item could be $10, but she ends up paying $10.80. Sometimes she has to pay $11.20 for the same price tag. To make it even more complicated, she sometimes has to pay the exact amount of the price tag. Johana wonders why she pays more than the price tag most of the time and how to calculate the extras.

Canadian governments (Federal, Provincial, and Municipal) charge you taxes for different reasons. Some of the most well-known taxes are the following:

- **Income Tax**: the tax that you pay for your income or revenue or salary
- **Sales Tax**: the tax that you pay when you purchase goods or services
- **Property Tax**: the tax that property owners need to pay
- **Excise Tax**: the tax that is embedded in the prices of some

products such as Alcoholic Beverages, Tobacco products, and Gasoline

I explain Sales Tax in this Tip. When you purchase a good or service, you need to pay an extra percentage on top of the original price to the merchant or service provider. The merchant in return needs to transfer the tax to the government.

GOODS AND SERVICES TAX (GST)

GST was first introduced by the former prime minister of Canada Brian Mulroney[31]. GST is a federal tax which is currently equivalent to 5% of the base price of some selected goods and services. For example, if you purchase children apparel, you need to pay this tax. If you purchase a child dress for the base price of $100, you need to pay $105 for the store. The amount of $5 is the GST. In Quebec "Revenu Québec" collects GST. "Canadian Revenue Agency" (CRA) is in charge of collecting GST for the rest of Canada.

Some goods and services are exempt from GST. In other words, the seller does not charge you GST for such goods and services. These products are called zero-rated goods and services. Visit the CRA website for a list of such products and services.

Unfortunately, the number of goods and services that are not exempt from GST is a lot more than those that are zero-rated.

PROVINCIAL SALES TAX (PST)

PST is also called the Retail Sales Tax (RST). In Quebec, this tax is called QST. The provincial governments collect this tax. Each province could charge consumers differently. The following list shows the current rates. The rates could change in the future.

- British Columbia 7%
- Alberta 0% (Alberta does not collect provincial sales tax)
- Manitoba 7%
- Quebec 7.5%
- Prince Edward Island (PEI) 10%
- Saskatchewan 5%

Provinces calculate PST on the original prices of the goods or services. The only exception is PEI which adds up GST first and then calculates PST.

For example, if a product is $100 and GST is 5%, then PEI tax would be $10.5 which is 10% of $105 (price + GST).

Four Canadian provinces Ontario, Newfoundland and Labrador, Nova Scotia, and New Brunswick do not collect PST. They instead collect HST or Harmonized Sales Tax which currently sits at 13%. I explain HST in the next section.

HARMONIZED SALES TAX (HST)

The Harmonized Sales Tax replaces the combination of GST and PST. For example, if you currently purchase an item in British Columbia with the original price of $100 you have to pay $5 for GST and $7 for PST which is confusing. To make matters worse there are some goods or services that only GST apply to them, or they are exempt from both GST and PST.

To simplify the matter, the Federal government encourages provinces to use HST which is a single tax that replaces both GST and PST. The current rate for HST is 13%. As I mentioned earlier, four of Canadian provinces use this method of sales taxation.

GST/HST CREDIT

If your annual income is below a certain level, then you are eligible for GST/ HST Credit. CRA (Canada Revenue Agency) issues monthly or quarterly cheques to those people who qualify. The intention is to compensate them for the GST or HST they have paid. If you are a newcomer to Canada it is very likely that you are eligible for GST/HST credit so, do not miss this opportunity. Visit the following link for more information.

settler.ca/88/gst

---

[31] https://en.wikipedia.org/wiki/Goods_and_services_tax_(Canada)

ABOUT PARSAI IMMIGRATION SERVICES

Parsai Immigration Services is in the Financial District of Toronto at the Sheraton Centre. We have helped thousands of applicants with their Canadian visa, eTA, study permit, work permit, immigration, and citizenship applications since January 2011. We are a proud member of the British Canadian Chamber of Trade and Commerce and Toronto Hispanic Chamber of Commerce. We are also a partner of many other organizations.

Al Parsai, the CEO of Parsai Immigration Services, is a Regulated Canadian Immigration Consultant and a member of CAPIC and ICCRC. He has represented thousands of clients from more than 35 countries to immigration authorities at the federal and provincial levels since January 2011. He is also a lecturer at Ashton College (Vancouver) and Global School of Corporate Excellence (Toronto). Al teaches immigration consulting courses to those who would like to become future immigration consultants. Al delivers workshops, seminars, and speeches for corporate clients and other immigration practitioners.

Al holds a master's degree in counselling psychology, a certificate with honours in the Immigration Consultant program, and a bachelor's degree in Mechanical Engineering. As a Regulated Canadian Immigration Consultant, Al strives to serve his clients to immigrate to Canada, sponsor loved ones, get study permits, get temporary work permits, and be represented at the Immigration Refugee Board hearings. Al has written more than 1100 articles or blog posts about immigration to Canada. Some of his articles have appeared on Canadian Immigrant and Newcomer magazines.

Parsai Immigration Services primarily operates in Ontario with several clients in other provinces of Canada and other countries. Our previous or existing clients are from Canada, China, Iran, Afghanistan, Hungary, Chile, Trinidad and Tobago, Japan, Norway, Germany, the United States, Spain, Ecuador, Ukraine, the United Kingdom, France, etc. If you can communicate and correspond in either English, French, Spanish, Urdu, or Persian languages, we'd be more than happy to assist you. Please visit us at settler.ca.

Printed in Great Britain
by Amazon